The Dunn Kitchen

DR. OETKER

GERMAN COOKING TODAY

THE ORIGINAL

DR. OETKER

GERMAN COOKING TODAY

THE ORIGINAL

 CERES

Unless otherwise stated the recipes in this book
are calculated for four portions.

We would like to thank the following
companies for providing props:

AEG, Nuremberg
Fürst-Bestecke, Solingen
Krafft GmbH, Steinenbronn
Hutschenreuther, Selb
AUBECQ, Auxe le Chateau

Copyright: © 1987 Ceres-Verlag
Rudolf-August Oetker KG, Bielefeld

Editor: Gisela Knutzen

Essential information: Christa Thim, Erlenbach

Recipe and text: Test kitchen, Dr. August Oetker, development Bielefeld
Headed by Lieselotte Kratschmer

Translation: W. B. Düchting, Düsseldorf

Cover and inside photography: Christiane Pries, Borgholzhausen

Reproductions: Pörtner & Saletzki, Bielefeld

Typesetting: Junfermann Druck & Service, Paderborn

Printing: Neue Stalling, Oldenburg

ISBN 3-7670-0364-3

Foreword

For many generations this tried and trusted standard work on German cookery has been the mainstay and reference book of both beginners and experienced housewives.

Throughout the years it has been continuously updated, taking account of new products and the latest developments in nutritional science. Its combination of the traditional and innovative makes it a contemporary classic.

Using the clear and concise texts and helpful step-by-step photos, both beginners and advanced cooks will have no problems in achieving the perfect results shown in the many beautiful colour photographs.

The expanded, richly illustrated, Essential Information section explains the principles of healthy eating, and tells the reader about new products, besides giving tips and tricks to ensure successful results with the individual recipes.

The motto of the new Dr. Oetker Basic Cookery Book is: cook, enjoy, be healthy.

Yours sincerely,
CERES-Verlag

Table of Contents

Table of Contents

Table of Contents

Table of Contents

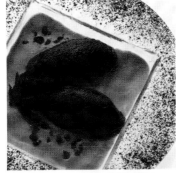
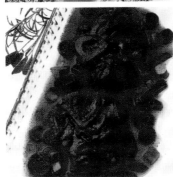

Nutrition Today

Nutrition Today

Virtually no area of human life is as important as nutrition. It is a major factor affecting our state of health. For many people, eating is one of life's great pleasures. However, in addition to the subjective aspects of enjoying our food, eating the "right" things plays a very important part in contributing to our physical well-being. A well balanced diet helps us to perform well and stay healthy. This chapter deals with the most important areas of nutritional science and explains their basic terminology. It also provides advice on the recommended way of going about things. There is no need to fill our kitchens with tables of nutritional values and other documents to consult during our daily cooking. It suffices to know the basic principles and rules and to stick to them wherever possible.

The most important thing is to have a varied diet. This means using the widest possible range of raw materials (foodstuffs) to ensure that we get an adequate quantity of nutrients and other essential ingredients. If, in addition to this, we take advantage of food which is in season at the relevant time of year, we can shop economically too.

The consensus of opinion is that daily food intake should be split up into 5 meals a day (three main meals and 2 snacks). In this way we assure a steady level of performance throughout the day. Generally speaking the following distribution can be recommended:

Breakfast and supper	25 % each
Snacks	10 % each
Midday meal	30 %

Energy Requirements

The energy requirement of an individual depends on his basal metabolism and his work energy. These two together show his actual daily energy requirement.

Basal metabolism
+ work energy
= total energy (daily energy)

Basal metabolism. This is the amount of energy consumed when resting (e.g. also during sleep).

Work energy. This is the additional energy needed for physical exertion. The different foods that the body receives provide it with different levels of energy. If both the amount of energy and the ratios of the individual nutrients are correct, this guarantees that in the long term, the body receives all of the necessary materials to maintain its functions.

Kilocalories/kilojoules

For some time now the energy content of all foodstuffs has been measured in **kilojoules**, an international measuring unit. This has taken over from the previously used kilocalorie unit.

Energy is measured:

1 kJ = 0.24 kcal
1 kcal = 4 kJ (4.184 to be precise)

To raise the temperature of 1 litre of water by 1 degree, you need 4.184 kJ (1 kcal).

Daily energy requirement for various activities (average values):
- Light, mainly sedentary, physical activity (e.g. secretary, laboratory assistant, chauffeur): 2200 kcal/day (= 9200 kJ).
- Medium physical activity (e.g. housewife with children, motor mechanic): 2800 kcal/day (= 11300 kJ).
- strenuous physical activity (e.g. bricklayer, carpenter, athlete): 3400 kcal/day (= 13800 kJ).
- very strenuous physical activity (e.g. forestry worker, quarry worker, top athlete): 3800 kcal/day (= 15900 kJ).

There is a rule of thumb by which to calculate the daily kilocalorie requirement of a person engaged in light physical activity:
ideal weight x 32 = daily kcal requirement,
i.e. a person with an ideal weight of 60 kg needs to take in 1920 kcal (= 8030 kJ) daily. A person with an ideal weight of 70 kg needs 2240 kcal per day (= 9370 kJ).

Ideal weight/normal weight
The number of centimetres a person is taller than one meter corresponds to his "normal weight" in kg. For example a person who is 1 meter and 70 centimetres tall would have a "normal weight" of 70 kg. "Ideal weight" is calculated as follows:

- For men, deduct 5% from the normal weight.
  70 kg − 5% = 66.5 kg.
- For women, deduct 10% from the normal weight.
  70 kg − 10% = 63 kg.

Recommended ratio of nutrients

12 − 15% protein
30 − 35% fat
55 − 60% carbohydrates

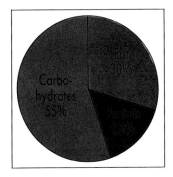

Example: A daily energy requirement of 2000 kcal should contain nutrients in the following proportions:
- Protein
  approx. 60.0 − 75.0 g
- Fat
  approx. 66.5 − 77.5 g
- Carbohydrates
  approx. 275.0 − 300.0 g

If we adhere to a really varied diet, based on the above values, we can be assured that our bodies are being supplied with the necessary vitamins, minerals and trace elements.

Nutrition Today

Energy content of the individual nutrients

1 gram of
- protein
  approx. 4 kcal
  = approx. 17 kJ
- fat
  approx. 9 kcal
  = approx. 38 kJ
- carbohydrate
  approx. 4 kcal
  = approx. 17 kJ
- alcohol
  approx. 7 kcal
  = approx. 29 kJ

When total energy is calculated, it is often forgotten that consumption of alcohol is a major factor in excessive calorie intake.

Protein

Protein is the primary source of growth for all cells and muscles in the human body. The individual cells in the human body are constantly being broken down and renewed. However, not all proteins are equally valuable. The various proteins are made up from more than 20 different building blocks, the amino acids. The body itself is unable to manufacture 8 of these amino acids and these must therefore be included in the diet. These are the so-called essential amino acids. The body is able to manufacture the remaining amino acids from other basic nutrients.

Recommended foodstuffs containing protein

Animal protein. High quantities are found in lean meat, poultry, game, fish, dairy produce, milk, eggs.

Vegetable protein. High quantities are found in grains, pulses-legumes, vegetables, nuts, almonds, potatoes.

Fats

These are our major suppliers of energy and a part of every cell in our bodies. They are also the carriers of vital, fat-soluble vitamins.
The human body contains fats in the form of neutral fats (combinations of glycerine and fatty acids) and lipoids (fat-like substances such as, for example, cholesterol). Fatty acids are the major ingredient in fats. We distinguish between mono-unsaturated, polyunsaturated and saturated fatty acids. Frequently the proportion of saturated fatty acids in the total fat intake is too high and should be reduced in favour of the polyunsaturated fatty acids.

Animal fats (butter, lard, suet) contain mainly saturated and mono-unsaturated fatty acids.

Polyunsaturated fatty acids are present in larger quantities in **vegetable fats** (e.g. sunflower, corn or thistle oils or margarines).
Our daily food intake contains both visible and invisible fats. We need **visible fats** for spreading and for the preparation of many types of food (see photo).

Invisible fats are contained in many individual raw materials and in prepared food, e.g. in meat, sausage, poultry, fish, milk and dairy produce, chocolate, mashed potato, cakes and biscuits.
It is easy to forget about the invisible fats in various foodstuffs. However, for anyone following a fat reduction diet, it is very important to take account of them.
Daily fat intake should under no circumstances exceed 1 g per kg of body weight. This means 60 g in the case of a normal weight of 60 kg. It must be remembered that around half of

this total fat is already "invisibly" present in many foodstuffs (see photo), so that only 30 g is available for spreading and food preparation.

Hints and tips to help cut down on fat

- Always measure fats exactly with a teaspoon or table-spoon.
  1 level teaspoon of fat is approximately equivalent to 4 – 5 g.
  1 level tablespoon of fat is approximately equivalent to 10 – 12 g.
- Butter and vegetable margarines contain less energy than cooking oil, since they contain only 80% fat. The rest is mainly water.
- Invisible fats mostly contain saturated fatty acids. There are some exceptions, e.g. almonds, nuts, avocados.
- Cooking methods that require little or no fat are preferable to those that need lots of fat (e.g. deep frying).

Carbohydrates

Carbohydrates are responsible for various metabolic processes. They make up more than half of our daily energy intake from food. Carbohydrates are usually divided into two groups:
Valuable carbohydrates, which supply the body not only with energy but also with nutrients, vitamins, trace elements, minerals and fibre. In addition, the body breaks them down more slowly, so that we feel hungry again less quickly. Photo 1, below, shows examples of foods that contain a high proportion of valuable carbohydrates: grains, wholegrain bread, crisp bread, fresh fruit, vegetables, dried fruit, potatoes and pulses-legumes.
Empty carbohydrates. These only supply energy, and most of them are quickly broken down. Photo 2, below, shows examples of foods that contain a high proportion of empty carbohydrates: white bread, toast, drinks containing sugar, sweetened jams, sweets, chocolate, highly sugared desserts, etc.

1

2

Nutrition Today

Fibre

Fibre is indigestible cellulose which provides the bulk or roughage needed to make the bowel work. It swells on contact with water and encourages bowel movement. In the modern diet the proportion of foodstuffs rich in fibre has decreased, so we generally ingest far too little. Foodstuffs which are rich in fibre are: pulses-legumes, wholegrain bread, grains generally, fresh fruit, vegetables, dried fruit. Foodstuffs that are low in fibre are: sweets, cake, white bread, toast, pasta made from plain white flour, meat, fish, eggs, sausage, dairy produce.

Vitamins and Minerals

Human life cannot exist without vitamins and minerals. They are a vital part of our diet and regulate many of our metabolic processes. Compared with other nutrients, we only need them in minute amounts, and they do not supply us with energy.

Vitamins are divided into the following groups:

- **Water-soluble** vitamins (all of the B-group vitamins and vitamin C)

- **Fat-soluble** vitamins (vitamins A, D, E and K).

Minerals are divided into the following groups:

- **Major elements**. These are required in larger quantities (e.g. calcium, phosphorous, magnesium, potassium).

- **Trace elements.** Only minute quantities of these are required (e.g. iron, tin, zinc, copper, manganese).

Vitamins and minerals fulfil totally different functions in the human body.

A few examples:

Vitamins and minerals are important for:

Vitamin B$_1$	breaking down carbohydrates
Vitamin D	storing minerals in the bones
Vitamin C	protection against infection
Vitamin A	ingredient of rhodopsin (eyes)
Iron	formation of red blood corpuscles
Iodine	thyroid gland function
Calcium	bone formation
Phosphorous	bone formation

The following foodstuffs have an especially high proportion of vitamins and minerals in varying ratios: Milk, dairy produce, fresh fruit, vegetables, bread, grains, wholegrain bread, meat, fish, potatoes, herbs, eggs. Many nutrients are lost by improper preparation or storage of food.

The measures shown below will help preserve valuable minerals and vitamins:

- Keep storage times as short as possible.
- Use fresh ingredients whenever possible.
- Do not chop food until after it has been washed.
- Use gentle cooking methods (e.g. sauting, steaming).
- Keep cooking times as short as possible.
- Do not keep prepared food warm for long periods.
- Eat fruit and vegetables raw whenever possible (but be sure to wash them carefully).
- To preserve food, freeze rather than sterilize.

Water

Most of the human body is made up of water. Without water there could be no life. All cells contain it, and it is an important transport medium and solvent for carrying nutrients and essential substances to their goals (cells, organs).

Our bodies need 2 to 2½ litres of water every day. We **take in water** by drinking, and by eating fruit and vegetables and food such as soups, sauces and casserole dishes.

We **expel water** in our urine and also through our skin (as perspiration), and by breathing.

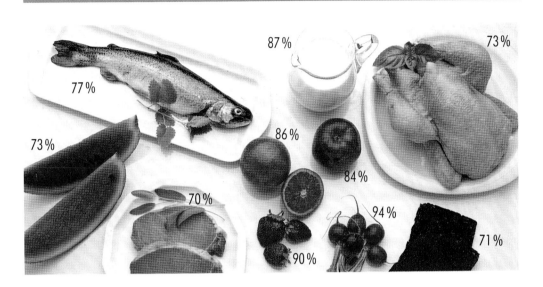

Proportion of water in various foodstuffs in %

Roasting chicken 73%
Water melon 73%
Oranges 86%
Radishes 94%
Milk 87%
Trout 77%
Pork schnitzel 70%
Wholegrain bread 71%
Strawberries 90%
Apples 84%

Wrong diet – a possible cause of diseases of civilization

An incorrect diet can encourage diet-related disease. Many people really want to eat a healthy diet, but the fact is that we still eat "too much", "too sweet", "not enough fibre" and "too fatty". In doing this we are laying a foundation for cardiovascular diseases, gout, diabetes, digestive problems, caries and obesity.

The following foodstuffs, if eaten to excess, will encourage the symptoms listed below:

Obesity: all foodstuffs that contain fat and sugar, sweets, cakes, soft drinks and cola, alcohol, sausage, fat cheese, spreading fat.

Increased blood pressure etc.: use of too much salt.

Increased uric acid levels in the body: meat, game, sausage, poultry, offal, fish, seafood, homemade stocks made from bones and meat.

Increased cholesterol or blood fat levels: fats such as, for example, too much coconut fat, butter, dripping, fat bacon etc., sausages, meat, game, fish, desserts, eggs, cakes.

Increased blood sugar levels: high consumption of easily resorbed, empty carbohydrates such as: sweets, sugar, honey, cakes, sweetened drinks and fruit preserves, ice-cream.

When putting together the daily menu it is particularly important to make sure that eating remains a pleasure. This means that we must take account of the basic principles of healthy nutrition. However, we will only be able to keep the family happy, if their meals taste good. The housewife who can combine a healthy diet and enjoyable meals will be doing the very best for her family in the long term. She will be helping them to enjoy their meals while keeping them healthy.

15

Using herbs and spices correctly

Herbs and spices give food that special something.

In times gone by spices were highly prized and valuable. They were sometimes weighed against gold, and were a privilege only the rich could afford. Nowadays they are available to everyone and a large selection can be found in any grocery store.

There is a growing choice of fresh herbs available on markets and in supermarkets. Nevertheless, the best herbs are always those grown in our own gardens or window boxes. Not only do herbs and spices allow us to bring variety to our daily menus, but they are also known for their therapeutic value in alleviating a whole range of diseases. They can have any of the following effects:

– stimulate appetite (e.g. rosemary, savory, basil);
– help cure a cold (e.g. sage);
– encourage perspiration (e.g. sage);
– improve circulation (e.g. rosemary);
– act as a diuretic (e.g. parsley, caraway, juniper, cress);
– improve digestion (e.g. caraway, ginger, aniseed).

If herbs and spices are used judiciously, it is possible to cut down on excessive use of salt.

Note:
Since cooking salt tends to spread quickly throughout a dish, it is advisable to use herbs and spices for flavouring and to add salt just before food is served.

Using spices

1. Spices must never mask the individual flavour of food. It is important to choose the right spice for each foodstuff.
2. Generally speaking, spices are added to food when cooking begins. This allows their aroma to permeate the raw ingredients better and means that the amount of salt used can be reduced dramatically.
3. Grind or pulverize spices just before they are needed (pepper mill, nutmeg grater, mortar and pestle, etc.). In this way, all their aroma and flavour are preserved.

Notes:
– Only buy ground spices in small quantities and store them separately in containers that are impermeable to air and light.
– Be careful with steam, spices can go lumpy and spoil.
– Be careful with hot fat, many spices can become bitter and burn (paprika).

A small selection from the large range of spices available

Pepper. The most important spice. The round fruits of the pepper bush. When the peppercorns have a green skin, they are unripe (preserved raw). Depending on how ripe peppercorns are, the skin can be red, black or a yellowish white. Black pepper is spicy and less ripe than mild white pepper.

Allspice: (Jamaica pepper). Round, red to dark brown berries which are picked before they are ripe. Dried and used whole or ground, e.g. for game, marinades, marinated beef, rice dishes, cakes and biscuits.

Curry: is a mixture of 12 – 15 different spices. Use for rice and grain dishes, poultry, fish, sauces.

Caraway: Whole or ground seeds. Use for cabbage, potatoes, minced meat, bread, quark.

Bay leaves: The dried leaves of the bay tree. Use for marinades, game, cabbage, pulses-legumes.

Nutmeg: Fruit of the evergreen nutmeg tree. For apple puree, mashed potato, brussels sprouts.

Cloves: Dried, whole or ground. Use for marinated beef, rice, millet, game, fruit puree, baking, mulled wine.

Paprika: Dried, ground pods. We distinguish between the sweet, slightly hot and very hot kinds.

Juniper: Violet berries of the juniper bush. For marinades, game, meat, fish, cabbage.

Vanilla: The scraped-out centre of the pod or the whole pod, cut into pieces, is used.

Cinnamon: The dried inner bark of the cinnamon tree. Ceylon cinnamon = spicy and mild, Kassia cinnamon (China) = very spicy.

Shopping for food

Shopping for a household needs careful planning. Good planning saves time and cuts costs.

Good planning means:

1. Preparing menus.
   Best done for a whole week in advance. In this way a list can be made that takes account of the household budget, the food you already have in stock, and foods that are in season.
2. Good store cupboard planning.
   Important foodstuffs that are needed constantly should always be in stock. Depending on your menu planning, these must be supplemented by additional ingredients. Avoid storing food for too long.
3. Keeping household accounts.
   Keep detailed notes on your shopping. In this way you will always know the exact status of your household budget and can avoid shortages.
4. Use convenience foods.
   Used properly, these will help save time and energy and will make your stock system efficient. The industry has taken a lot of dreary, time-consuming work out of our hands.

Points to note when shopping:

- Make a shopping list and stick to it. This saves you from impulse buying.
- Choose only the very freshest of food.
- Carefully check the "use by" date.
- Compare prices. Take advantage of special offers (first think about whether you can store them).
- Look critically at special offers. They are not always the best buy.
- When buying convenience foods, take a look at the list of ingredients. The raw ingredients are listed in order of decreasing weight ratio.

Stocks and storage

All food should be prepared when it is as fresh as possible. However it is advisable to have an emergency stock to cover about two weeks.

Advantages of storing food

- Food stays fresh longer in the fridge and freezer.
- Increased efficiency as daily shopping is no longer necessary.
- More efficient shopping for small households. Less wastage from bigger packs, e.g. cream or milk.
- Advantage can be taken of special offers (e.g. larger quantities of meat or vegetables can be bought and correctly frozen).
- Possibility of preparing dishes that are out of season.
- Reserves in case of illness or when guests come unexpectedly.

Storing food in the cellar

The cellar must be dark and well ventilated.
Best temperature:
- Earth floor +12°C.
- Cement floor +9° to +15°C.

Fruit and potatoes should be stored in appropriate wooden containers.

Storing long life foods in pantries or food cupboards
Pantries and food cupboards should be well ventilated. They should not be warmer than +15° to +20°C.

Storage times, unless otherwise indicated by the manufacturer ("use by" date):

Food	Years
Tinned fish	1–2
Tinned meat	3–5
Tinned soup	1–2
Tinned vegetables	2
Tinned fruit	1–2
Spices	1
Semolina, barley	½
Oats	½–1
Honey	1
Pulses-legumes	1
Coffee	1
Cocoa	½
Condensed milk	1
Jam	1–2
Flour	½
Rice	1
Cooking oil	1
Cornflour	1
Tea	½–1
Pasta	½–1
Dried fruit	1
Packet soups	¾–1
Rusks	1

Sugar, unlimited if kept dry.

Storing food in the fridge:
Best temperature: +2° – +4°C.

A few hints
- Allow cooked food to cool off first.
- Cover food to prevent it from drying out and passing its odour to other food stored in the fridge.
- Pour opened condensed milk into a jug before putting into the fridge.

- Store fruit and vegetables in the appropriate drawer. They will stay fresh longer that way.
- Remove mushrooms from their packing. They must be stored cool and dry.

Storage time in the fridge

Food	Days
Meat, raw	2–5
Meat, cooked	2–6
Minced meat, raw	6–8 **hours**
Minced meat, cooked	2–4
Sausage, fresh	1–4
Fish, raw	up to 24 hours
Fish, cooked	2–3
Milk, cream	4–5
Yoghurt	4–6
Cottage cheese	4–5
Hard cheese	10–14
Eggs	3–4 weeks
Vegetables, raw	3–8
Salads	1–3
Vegetables, cooked	1–3
Berries	2–10
Fruit, fresh	3–10
Pasta, cooked	2–4
Rice, cooked	2–4
Potato salad	up to 1

Note:
For freezer storage see page 29.

19

Table of nutritional values Food

100 g contain (bought raw food)	Protein g	Fat g	Carbo-hydrates g	Kilo-joules kJ	Kilo-calories kcal	Choles-terol
Beef:						
Fillet	19.2	4.4	—	527	126	70.0
Leg	17.4	5.9	—	552	132	99.6
Oxtail	21.0	11.5	—	770	184	70.0
Sirloin	19.0	9.4	—	724	173	64.4
Tongue	11.8	11.8	—	699	167	79.9
Pork:						
Fillet	18.6	9.9	—	736	176	70.0
Minced (half and half)	20.0	20.0	—	1088	260	70.0
Smoked loin	17.3	14.1	—	920	220	—
Leg	15.2	20.6	—	1100	263	63.0
Chops	13.1	19.6	—	1021	244	56.0
Liver	20.1	5.7	1.1	615	147	346.0
Kidneys	14.4	4.5	0.7	456	109	305.0
Veal:						
Breast	10.6	3.6	—	339	81	51.3
Leg	16.1	1.2	—	347	83	70.0
Shoulder	15.8	2.2	—	381	91	69.3
Mutton:						
Chops	16.9	2.4	—	410	98	54.6
Poultry:						
Duck	14.5	13.8	—	812	194	60.0
Goose	9.9	19.5	—	958	229	55.0
Roasting chicken	15.2	4.1	—	448	107	56.0
Turkey (steak)	24.1	1.0	—	481	115	0.0
Boiling fowl	13.5	14.8	—	837	200	55.0
Game:						
Rabbit	16.4	6.0	—	552	132	55.3
Venison	15.7	2.5	—	389	93	77.0
Leg of wild boar	18.8	2.1	—	410	98	0.0
Fish:						
Eel (fresh)	10.5	17.2	—	874	209	99.4
Trout	10.1	1.4	—	243	58	28.6
Haddock (net)	17.7	0.4	—	343	82	30.0
Redfish	8.7	1.7	—	230	55	18.2
Coley	11.9	0.5	—	238	57	21.5
Plaice, fillets	17.1	0.8	—	343	82	50.0
Dairy produce:						
Butter milk	3.5	0.5	4.0	151	36	4.0
Crème fraîche. 30% fat	2.6	30.2	3.9	1293	309	0.0
Yoghurt, 3.5% fat	3.9	3.8	4.6	293	70	10.0
Double cream, 30% fat	2.4	31.7	3.4	1326	317	109.0
Sour cream, 10% fat	3.1	10.5	4.0	531	127	34.0
Milk, 3.5% fat	3.3	3.6	4.7	276	66	11.7
Eggs:						
Egg, class 3 (gross)	11.3	9.9	0.6	615	147	512.0
Oils and fats:						
Butter	0.7	83.2	0.7	3247	776	240.0
Margarine	0.2	80.0	0.4	3138	750	0.0
Peanut fat	—	93.0	—	3619	865	0.0
Vegetable oil	—	93.0	—	3619	865	0.0

100 g contain (bought raw food)	Protein g	Fat g	Carbo-hydrates g	Kilo-joules kJ	Kilo-calories kcal	Choles-terol
Grain produce:						
Semolina	10.3	0.8	75.3	1548	370	0.0
Rice, polished	7.0	1.0	79.0	1540	368	0.0
Sago	2.0	—	82.0	1435	343	0.0
Pasta	13.0	2.9	72.4	1632	390	0.0
Plain white flour	10.6	1.0	74.0	1540	368	0.0
Corn flour	0.4	0.1	86.6	1460	349	0.0
Oats (wholegrain)	13.5	7.0	66.4	1695	405	0.0
Vegetables:						
Cauliflower	1.6	0.2	2.4	71	17	0.0
Beans, French	2.3	0.2	4.8	134	32	0.0
Mushrooms	2.7	0.2	2.9	100	24	0.0
Chicory	1.2	0.2	2.0	59	14	0.0
Cucumber	0.4	0.1	1.0	29	7	0.0
Curly kale	2.2	0.5	2.6	100	24	0.0
Potatoes	1.6	0.1	14.8	293	70	0.0
Lettuce	1.3	0.2	2.2	67	16	0.0
Carrots	0.8	0.2	7.1	138	33	0.0
Chanterelles	1.0	0.3	1.8	59	14	0.0
Asparagus	1.4	0.1	2.2	63	15	0.0
Spinach	2.1	0.3	2.9	92	22	0.0
Tomatoes	0.9	0.2	3.3	79	19	0.0
Cabbage	1.1	0.2	3.3	79	19	0.0
Onions	1.2	0.2	8.0	176	42	0.0
Pulses:						
Beans (haricot)	21.3	1.6	57.6	1473	352	—
Peas	22.9	1.4	58.9	1515	362	—
Lentils	23.9	1.4	56.2	1481	354	—
Sweets:						
Sugar	—	—	99.8	1648	394	0.0
Chocolate (dairy milk)	9.1	32.8	54.7	2356	563	0.0
Fruit:						
Pineapple	0.3	0.1	7.1	126	30	0.0
Apples	0.3	0.4	12.6	230	55	0.0
Bananas	0.8	0.1	15.6	276	66	0.0
Pears	0.4	0.3	11.9	218	52	0.0
Strawberries	0.8	0.4	7.3	151	36	0.0
Raspberries	1.3	0.3	8.1	167	40	0.0
Plums	0.6	0.2	13.6	243	58	0.0
Grapes	0.7	0.3	16.1	289	69	0.0
Dried fruit	2.8	0.6	64.1	1151	275	0.0
Beverages:						
Apple juice	—	—	11.6	192	46	0.0
Orange juice, fresh	0.7	—	10.6	192	46	0.0
		Alcohol-content g				
Red wine, light	0.2	7.9	2.4	276	66	0.0
White wine, medium	0.2	8.4	2.6	293	70	0.0
Beer, pale	0.5	3.6	4.8	197	47	0.0

— = no data;   0 = non existent.

Cooking Methods

There are a variety of cooking methods that can be used to suit the type of food we are cooking. Nowadays there is an increasing trend towards using as little fat as possible for cooking. This has put more emphasis on aluminium foil, roasting bags and oven bricks. Even with conventional cooking methods such as baking and roasting it is possible to use very little fat.

Boiling

Cooking in a large quantity of simmering liquid (see Essential Information/Meat, page 94).

Pot roasting

This method involves frying food quickly in hot fat and then allowing cooking to continue in a covered pan in simmering liquid and steam (see Essential Information/Meat, page 94).

Shallow Frying/ Roasting

- Shallow Frying **in a frying pan.** Cooking and browning in a little fat (see Essential Information/Meat, page 94).
- Roasting **in the oven.** Browning and cooking in an open tin or pan (see Essential Information/Meat, page 95).

Steaming

Food is cooked in hot vapour at temperatures between 80° and 100°C.

During steaming the food is placed in the upper section of a steamer and cooks gently in the steam produced by the boiling water in the lower section. Steamed food is easily digestible and keeps its fresh colour and individual flavour. When steaming is finished, the flavorsome steaming liquid can be used for soups and sauces.

Tip: Add herbs and spices to the steaming liquid. Their aroma and flavour is transferred to the food being steamed.

Braising

Cooking in a little water and water vapour at temperatures under 100°C (see Essential Information/Vegetables, page 160).

Aluminium Foil

Food is cooked in its own juices (without browning).

Aluminium foil is very thinly rolled aluminium. Food cooked in this way keeps its flavour, vitamins and minerals. Aluminium imparts no taste or odour and is impermeable to liquid.

Important Notes:
- Lightly oil the foil to stop food from sticking.
- Fold the foil correctly to prevent any liquid from escaping. Make a letter, block or bag shape (see photo above).
- Do not wrap the foil too tightly around the food as there must be enough space for steam to develop.
- Place sealed foil packages on the wire oven shelf (possibly in an ovenproof dish), as the bottom of the oven is too hot and the foil will stick to it.
- Cooking times will increase by about ⅓ compared with normal cooking times.

Deep Frying

Cooking and browning food by immersing it in hot fat at temperatures between 170°C and 180°C.

This is a fast method of cooking in which food is browned evenly on all sides (e.g. chips, croquettes, coated fish or meat portions, doughnuts). Deep frying requires a lot of fat, and should be used as little as possible.

Roasting bags/tubes

Food is cooked and browned in its own juices.

As opposed to food cooked in aluminium foil, food cooked in roasting bags does brown in the radiant heat. Roasting bags are heat resistant in temperatures of up to 230°C and are only suitable for preparing food in the oven.

They are made from a neutral synthetic material and are sold in the form of bags and tubes as well as by the roll, and are sealed with aluminium strips.

Important notes:

- "Put in food" seal bag/tube.

- Do not wrap the bag/tube too tightly around the food. There must be enough space for steam to develop.

- Prick a few holes in the bag/tube (see photo above) to allow steam to escape.

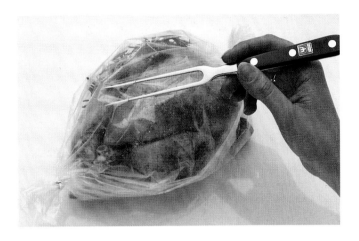

- Place the bag/tube on the **cold** wire shelf. It would burst immediately if placed on the hot shelf.
- Make sure the bag/tube is not too close to the sides or top of the oven. It could expand and stick to them.

Grilling

Cooking and browning under radiant heat at very high temperatures. This method of cooking uses very little fat.

Important notes:

- Food that has been marinated (oil, marinade, spices) is more tender, as well as tastier.

- First mix the spices with the oil and then brush the food with the mixture. The spices cannot burn (see photo below).
  Salt after cooking.

- When grilling over charcoal, it is advisable to place food on aluminium foil or in special grilling dishes.

Pressure Cooking

Pressure cooking considerably shortens cooking times in comparison with other methods. The food is placed in a hermetically sealed pan which is then pressurized. When the liquid inside the pan is heated, pressure builds up and the temperature inside the pan is raised to above 100°C.

The food is cooked at temperatures between 108° and 118°C. The high temperature means that cooking time can be reduced by about ⅔.

Pressure cookers have a valve (fixed or screw-on) either in the lid or handle, which is pushed up as the pressure inside the pan rises. The valve has markings

which indicate the temperature inside the pan.

When the desired temperature has been reached the cooking time starts. This cooking time must be stringently adhered to, otherwise food will be overcooked. If the pressure inside the pan becomes too high, the valve automatically opens to allow the excess pressure to escape.

Pressure cooking is especially valuable for food that needs long cooking, e.g. pulses, boiling meat, boiling fowl. Food that needs a strong sauce is first fried on a high heat. When the desired degree of browning has been achieved, liquid is added and cooking is continued under pressure (e.g. beef olives, goulash, braised beef).

Important notes:
– Always clean the valve carefully to ensure a correct temperature reading.
– ⅛ litre of liquid is needed to produce sufficient steam.
– Never fill the pan more than ⅔ full.
– Automatic hotplates are not suitable for pressure cooking as they increase the cooking time.
– Never open the pan when it is under pressure.

Oven Brick

Food is cooked in its own juices (with or without browning). This is a gentle method of cooking which requires little fat. The brick is made of porous clay and must be immersed in water for about 15 minutes before use (see photo below), to saturate it with water. The brick is then placed into the **cold** oven. During cooking the brick releases the water it has absorbed as steam. Food stays juicy and is cooked gently.

Important notes:
– No fat needed.
– **Always** water the brick before putting it into the **cold** oven.
– Oven bricks can shatter if subjected to large variations in temperature.
  – For example, place the hot brick onto a wooden board.
  – Do not add cold liquid to the hot brick.
– Wash in hot water containing no washing-up liquid.
– Leave brick to dry thoroughly in a well ventilated place.

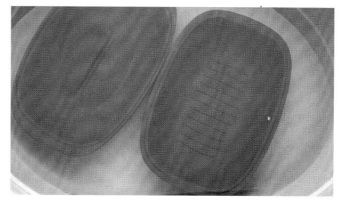

Abbreviations

kg = kilogram
g = gram
l = litre
ml = millilitre
dl = decilitre
cl = centilitre
tbs = tablespoon

tsp = teaspoon
lev. = level
kJ = kilojoule
kcal = kilocalorie
P = protein
F = fat
Ch = carbohydrate
F.i.d. = fat in dry mass

Volume and weight equivalents

1000 ml (1 l)	water =	1 kg	= 1000 g
750 ml (¾ l)	water =	¾ kg	= 750 g
500 ml (½ l)	water =	½ kg	= 500 g
375 ml (⅜ l)	water =	⅜ kg	= 375 g
250 ml (¼ l)	water =	¼ kg	= 250 g = soup plate
125 ml (⅛ l)	water =	125 g	= approx. 8 tbs
100 ml (1/10 l)	water =	100 g	= 1 dl = just 7 tbs
15 ml	water =	1 tbs	= 15 g
10 ml	water =	1 cl	= 10 g

The measures shown are average measures, in view of the large variety of spoon shapes found in kitchens.

Foodstuff	1 level tsp	1 level tsp
Baking powder	3 g	10 g
Crème fraîche	5 g	15 g
Fat	5 g	15 g
Semolina	3 g	12 g
Oats	2 g	8 g
Honey	6 g	20 g
Yoghurt	6 g	17 g
Cocoa, soluble	2 g	6 g
Almonds, ground	3 g	8 g
Flour	3 g	10 g
Horseradish	6 g	20 g
Nuts, ground	3 g	8 g
Oil	4 g	12 g
Salad cream	5 g	15 g
Salt	5 g	15 g
Sour cream	6 g	17 g
Double cream	5 g	15 g
Breadcrumbs	3 g	10 g
Mustard	3 g	9 g
Cornflour	3 g	9 g
Tomato ketchup	5 g	19 g
Tomato pure	5 g	18 g
Sugar	5 g	15 g

Quantities

The following quantities are average quantities per portion. In individual households these will have to be adjusted to meet the personal situation and specific requirements. Age, type of work, habits and combinations of foodstuffs must be taken into account. Generally speaking a meal is based on the following quantities per person.

Soup starter: 150 – 200 ml

Main course:
Casserole-soup 375 – 500 ml
Meat 100 – 125 g
Meat, with bone 125 – 150 g
Fish fillet 100 – 150 g
– on the bone 150 – 200 g

Accompaniments:
Sauce approx. 100 ml
Vegetables (cleaned) 200 g
Salad (cleaned) 40 – 50 g
Potatoes (peeled) 200 g
Rice, millet, barley, etc. 50 g (raw)
Pasta 50 g (raw)
Dried fruit 60 g

Dessert:
Fresh fruit 150 – 200 g
Fruit puree 150 g

Glossary of Kitchen Terms

Bake: To cook and brown in dry, hot air at various temperatures (mainly cake, sweet or savoury).

Bake blind: To bake or pre-bake a pastry case without a filling.

Bard: To cover or wrap lean meat or poultry in thin slices of bacon or pork back fat.

Beat, aerate: To work air into food, e.g. cream or egg whites.

Blanch: To plunge food into boiling water for a specified period of time, and then cool it quickly in ice water.

Boil: To cook food in a large quantity of liquid at a temperature of around 100C.

Bone: To remove the bones from fresh game, meat or poultry.

Braise: To cook food in a little of its own or added liquid, with or without the addition of fat (e.g. vegetables).

Carve: To cut whole animals or large joints of meat into portions.

Clarify: To bind and remove impurities using a little whisked egg white, e.g. for stock, heat slowly and sieve.

Clean: To remove all inedible parts from food, e.g. wilted leaves or hard areas from vegetables.

Coat: To cover food first in flour, then in egg and then in breadcrumbs, ground nuts, desiccated coconut, etc. before frying it.

Curdle: To stiffen a beaten egg mass, e.g. in a water bath, hot air (oven) or pan.

Cut: To reduce food in size by chopping it with a sharp knife, e.g. into strips, diamond shapes, slices, dice.

Cut up: To cut raw or cooked food into slices or portions.

Deep Fry: To cook and brown food by immersing it in hot fat.

Degrease: To remove the fat from the top of sauces or soups.

Draw: To remove the intestines of poultry and fish.

Dress: To use skewers, clips or thread to hold food that is ready to cook in the required shape (e.g. beef olives, stuffed poultry).

Farce: French term for very fine forcemeat stuffing, e.g. meat, fish or mushroom farce.

Fillet: To remove the head, skin and bones from raw food while cutting it into pieces.

Flame: To set alight a small amount of warmed spirit which has been poured over food.

Flour: To turn dry food in flour before frying it, e.g. liver, schnitzels.

Fold in: To gently mix one mass with another without stirring, e.g. folding beaten egg white into a sponge mixture.

Grate: To break down food into small or large particles by rubbing across a grater.

Gratinate: To brown the surface of a dish by applying strong heat from above.

Grill: To cook and brown by means of radiant or contact heat.

Grind: To reduce hard raw ingredients between grindstones or rollers, e.g. pepper, nutmeg, poppy seeds or coffee.

Hang: Some game and meat needs to be hung in a cool place for a time to tenderize it before it is cooked.

Knead: To make a dough by applying pressure to mix together food of different consistencies.

Liaison: A thickener of egg yolk, cream or butter, which is added to a liquid no longer on the boil.

Marinate: To soak food in a mixture of vinegar, wine or buttermilk with herbs and spices.

Melt: To liquefy solid food by the application of low heat (e.g. gelatine, chocolate, fat).

Mince: To chop food by putting it through a meat grinder.

Peel: To remove the skin from food, e.g. potatoes, cucumbers, bananas.

Pipe: To extrude a creamy mass from a piping bag into a specific shape (e.g. choux pastry, whipped egg whites, icing).

Poach: To cook food in a small or large quantity of barely simmering liquid.

Preserve: To place food into a specific liquid, e.g. alcohol, vinegar, citric acid solution, salt or sugar solution, to preserve it.

Puree, mash: To mash or beat soft raw or cooked food to a fine consistency.

Refresh: To rinse freshly cooked hot food briefly under cold water.

Reheat: To warm up cold cooked food or drink.

Render: To heat small pieces of fatty food to extract the fat.

Roast: To cook and brown raw food in the oven with or without the addition of fat.

Roll out: To roll out pastry in all directions on a pastry board, with a rolling pin.

Scale: To remove the scales from fish.

Season: To add herbs, spices or salt to food.

Sieve: To separate liquids and solids by pouring them through a sieve (e.g. for sauces).

Singe off: To remove any remaining feathers or quills from poultry, by holding the bird over a naked flame.

Skim: To remove the foam or scum which forms after a first boiling (congealed protein), e.g. when making stock, heating butter or cooking fruit.

Squeeze: To separate liquid and solid parts of food using pressure, e.g. to obtain juice.

Steam: To cook food in water vapour.

Stew: To brown food in hot fat before cooking it in a small amount of simmering liquid in a covered container.

Stir: To make ingredients, sometimes of various consistencies, homogeneous by stirring.

Strain: To press or stroke soft raw or cooked ingredients through a sieve.

Swell: To allow rice or pasta to increase in volume by absorbing liquid.

Thaw: To thaw frozen food in the correct manner.

Thicken: To add a thickening agent to liquids.

Thicken, reduce: To thicken a liquid by boiling it down and evaporating the more volatile component.

Water: To soak in water, e.g. herrings.

Freezing Food

Freezing is a method of preserving food. The most important thing to remember is that food should be fast frozen. This means that most of the moisture in the cells of the food is frozen so quickly at -30°C that only small ice crystals form. If the freezing temperature is not low enough, larger ice crystals form, and these change and destroy the structure of the cells. This spoils the appearance of the food when it is thawed and reduces its nutritional value.

Important notes:

- Switch your freezer on to fast freeze some time before you are ready to fill it.

- Freeze only fresh or freshly cooked food.

- Allow cooked food to cool off before freezing.

- Lean food can be kept longer than fatty food.

- Food should not be seasoned, salted or sugared until it has thawed. Salt and sugar draw out the juices from food; spices lose their depth of flavour.

- Spread berries on trays to fast freeze them before packing as usual.

- Pack your freezer neatly and label everything. In this way you can quickly find what you need and the freezer can be shut again quickly (frost formation).

- Blanch vegetables, otherwise the protein will break down (especially important for peas and beans). Put vegetables in a wire basket and immerse in a pan of boiling water for 2–4 minutes. Plunge into ice water to cool off.

- Packing materials must be acid resistant, cold resistant, impermeable to air and strong (e.g. extra strong aluminium foil, freezer bags, boxes, boiling bags, aluminium dishes).

- Label packages, giving the contents and the date when the food was packed (see photo on right).
- Use easily stackable containers with a well fitting lid.
- Fill containers containing **no** liquid (e.g. vegetables) to the rim. Containers containing liquid (e.g. soup) should only be filled to within 2 cm of the rim (the liquid expands during freezing).
- Food that has been placed in the freezer to freeze should not touch other food. This permits the cold to penetrate the food better. When frozen the food may be stacked.

The following foods are unsuitable for freezing:

(Examples)
- Thickened sauces
- Custards
- Gelatine dishes without egg and cream
- Yoghurt
- Cheese (loss of aroma)
- Salad, radishes, potatoes.

Thawing poultry and meat

1. Remove the food from the container.
2. Leave it to thaw in a container with a perforated insert, or lay it on an upturned soup plate. Food that is thawing must **not** be allowed to lie in the thawing liquid.
3. Discard any thawing liquid.

Other notes:
- It is not necessary to thaw vegetables before using them.
- Small portions of meat or fish can be used when slightly thawed.
- Meat that is only slightly or not fully thawed cuts easily, e.g. for goulash or fricassee.
- Food that has been frozen in boiling bags can be thawed in a water bath.
- Thaw **cooked** dumplings in the top section of a steamer in water vapour.
  Raw dumplings should be removed from their packing and thawed and cooked in simmering water.

Freezer storage times

Temperature
from -18° to -20°C

Food	No. of months
Beef, lean	2 – 9
Pork	4 – 5
Lamb, lean	6 – 10
Game	9 – 12
Chicken	8 – 10
Duck	4 – 6
Wildfowl	8 – 10
Sausage	2 – 4
Fish	2 – 4
Egg yolk	8 – 10
Egg white	10 – 12
Butter/margarine	6 – 8
Vegetables	6 – 8
Fruit	8 – 10
Bread	4 – 6
Bread rolls	2 – 4
Small cakes, baked	4 – 6
Gateaux	2 – 3
Yeast dough, unbaked	8 weeks
Cooked food	2 – 3

Types of energy: Gas, electricity/convection heat

The development of cooker hobs

In the past most cooking was done with gas. Cooking with gas has many advantages, e.g. the immediate availability of full heat, infinitely adjustable gas jets and simple adjustment of the open flame to the size of the pan.

However, cooking by electricity has become increasingly popular. Reasons: it is easier to connect to the mains supply in the case of fitted kitchens and less dangerous to use. There have been major developments in the construction of electric hotplates. Nowadays, in addition to the standard type of burner, we have cookers with ceramic hobs, radiant heat and radiant heat with halogen light. The latest innovation is the induction hob. These are faster and more economical than previous hobs.

Burner settings

Setting	Use for:
0	Burner is off.
½	Keep food warm.
1	Simmer after boiling; braising; steaming; stewing small quantities; thawing frozen food.
1½	Cooking larger quantities of food; Slow frying in little fat.
2	Frying; stewing; deep frying.
2½	Sear food to seal pores.
3	Bringing to the boil quickly.

Fast and superfast burners.

These are usually marked with a red spot. They heat up more quickly and are therefore suitable for bringing liquid to the boil quickly, boiling up and searing food.

Automatic burner

Setting	Use for:
0	Burner is off.
1	Melting, dissolving gelatine.
2 – 3	Keeping food warm, swelling; heating milk.
4 – 5	Braising; steaming; thawing frozen food.
6 – 7	Frying in little fat; stewing larger amounts of food.
8 – 9	Quick, gentle frying.
9 – 10	Frying; pot-roasting larger pieces of meat.
11 – 12	Bringing liquid to the boil, deep frying.

AEG have introduced a new automatic burner, the Regla-90-automatic burner, which is very practical. Once it has been set, it automatically switches from a high starting temperature to a lower simmering temperature.

Induction hobs

This is the very latest in high technology (see AEG induction hob in photo below). When cooking by induction, the heat is produced directly in the base of the pan by means of electromagnetic exchange fields. This means that heat is produced only where it is needed. It is no longer necessary to heat the pan through the medium of the burner (see example in photo below).

When liquid is being heated, the temperature of the ceramic glass hob stays so low that the lace doily is not damaged.

The advantages of this new heating method are its fast reaction time and great safety, e.g. the ceramic glass hob around the burner remains virtually cold. The induction burner recognizes the right pan and switches itself off in case of overheating.

The development of cooker ovens

Gas ovens were widely distributed in years gone by, but were difficult to regulate by way of the constantly burning jets. Nowadays most cooks prefer electric ovens.

Ovens with hot air systems

An intensive stream of hot air surrounds the food and cooks it. The air is heated and continually circulated around the oven. This system permits food to be cooked simultaneously on all of the oven shelves. The temperature ranges vary from model to model. Read your instructions carefully.

Ovens with conventional heating

In this form of heating, the heat is produced at the top and bottom of the oven and is radiated to the food.

Temperature settings

Gas	Electricity	Use for:
	50 °C	Proving yeast dough
	75 °C	Keeping food warm, warming crockery
1	100 – 125 °C	Slow drying biscuits (macaroons)
2	175 °C	Sterilizing (preserving)
2	175 – 190 °C	High cakes (madeira cake)
3	200 °C	Medium cakes (yeastcake), casseroles, baked dishes, pot roasts
3 – 4	210 – 225 °C	Flat cakes, large joints of meat
5 – 6	225 – 250 °C	Flat joints of meat, gratinating

Multiple choice ovens

The latest ovens can be switched to any of 4 types of heating:

– **Four-shelf hot-air system**
For large quantities.
– **Top and bottom heat**
For specific recipes
– **Grill**
Flat pieces of food are grilled by radiant heat" the surface becomes crisp.
– **Infratherm grill**
Hot air is circulated around the food being grilled. The food is browned without the use of additional implements to turn it. This is especially useful for large joints of meat and poultry.

A further major improvement is offered by AEG VITRATHERM fitted ovens. In these the top and bottom heating elements are fitted behind transparent ceramic glass panels. Advantages: easier to clean, and a large grill surface for better grilling results.

Microwave ovens

Perhaps you already own a microwave oven, or if not, you have almost certainly read or heard all about them. Let's face it, microwave ovens are ahead of the trend, and there are a lot of reasons why this is so.

What are microwaves and how do they work?

A microwave oven is the ideal adjunct to your conventional cooker and oven. There is no question of it replacing them. Its greatest strengths lie in thawing, heating and cooking food. Basically a microwave oven is composed of two parts; the cooking compartment with metal walls, which may have an additional synthetic covering, and the electrical part containing the magnetron. The magnetron converts the electricity into microwaves. These are electromagnetic waves which are distributed throughout the cooking compartment by means of a stirrer, a reflector or a turntable. Microwaves cannot penetrate metal; they bounce of the walls, ceiling and floor of the oven, hit the food, penetrate it and start its molecules vibrating. This creates friction and friction creates heat. In this way the food is heated, thawed or cooked – quickly too, for the molecules vibrate 2.5 billion times per second.

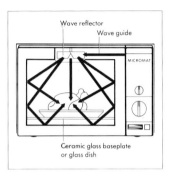

Microwave energy creates heat in all organic materials. In fact, it is used in medicine for this very reason, to give patients heat treatment.

What should a microwave oven have?

A microwave oven should have a multi-step or infinitely variable choice of settings. This allows the correct setting to be chosen for every type of food in any quantity. In addition a microwave oven should have an electronic timer, or at least an electromechanical timer, for exact setting of short cooking times. It must be possible to set this timer for exact ½ to 1 minute intervals in the short 1-5 minute range.

Typical examples from the AEG range of microwave ovens:

The Micromat FX 179 L, in dark brown, has 10 settings from 10% to 100%. Data input is easy, via touch foil. It has an electronic timer and can be programmed to run 3 different preset settings automatically.

What are the advantages of a microwave oven?

To be able to make the best possible use of your microwave oven it is important to understand the principles on which it works. Your microwave oven can become an ideal adjunct to your conventional cooker, i.e. while your are baking or grilling food in your conventional cooker, you can be quickly and economically thawing, heating or cooking food in the microwave oven.

Here are a few examples:

– Because cooking is gentle and short, and only a little or no liquid is used, food retains most of its important nutrients. Its natural colour and taste are hardly altered.
– Food can be put on to plates and heated individually, as required. Reheating is gentle, and food tastes freshly cooked.
– You need less utensils, since most food can be served in the utensil it is cooked in.

The Micromat FX 24 X, in white, has 600 watts and 4 settings. It has a 60 minute timer with a special short time range and gives an audible signal when the set time has run out. The light, generously proportioned, 20 litre cooking compartment has a door which opens downwards.

Where to keep your microwave oven?

Microwave ovens can be kept freestanding on a work surface or can be built into cupboards or attached to the bottom of wall cupboards. The example below shows the UX-112 Z oven by AEG.

Basic Kitchen Equipment

Essential kitchen tools

A good selection of kitchen knives is very important. These are in daily use and should therefore be of the best quality. The blades should be made from good quality steel to ensure that they do their job well over a long period of time. A good knife should feel secure and comfortable in the hand. The following basic equipment should be present in an efficiently run kitchen:

General kitchen knife and **potato peeler** for peeling and trimming fruit and vegetables. Available in many shapes and sizes.

A **meat knife,** short or long, to cut raw or cooked meat evenly.

A **carving knife and fork,** – a fork with two long prongs and a long, sharp knife. Essential for slicing large joints of meat and poultry.

Kitchen scissors are an all purpose item. They can be used to open packages or cut up kitchen herbs. The cavity behind the blades is to open difficult screw tops and lift off crown corks.

Poultry shears are strong, and have sharp blades. With them you can cut raw and cooked poultry into portions. They are strong enough to cut through poultry bones.

Double-handed herb chopper; its curved blades are used in a rocking action to chop herbs, vegetables, meat and fish, both raw and cooked.

The **garlic press** is used to crush peeled cloves of garlic into very fine pieces.

A 2–4 person household should have the following utensils:
- 1 small and 1 large casserole
- 1 stewing pan
- 1 saucepan
- 1 set of bowls
- 1 long and 1 oval baking dish
- 1 small and 1 large frying pan
- 1 timer
- 1 measuring jug

In addition, an efficient kitchen should also contain the following:

- 1 electric mixer with accessories
- 2–3 large and small cutting boards in wood, plastic or marble
- 1 set of scales
- 1–2 heat-proof stands
- a variety of baking tins
- 1 tray
- 1 cake rack
- 1 bread basket
- 1 potato press
- 1 multi-purpose vegetable grater
- 1 rolling pin and 1 pastry scraper

- 1 salad drying basket and 1 tea sieve
- 1 set of salad servers
- 1 turner
- 1 ladle
- 1 wooden spoon
- 1 gravy spoon
- 1 slotted spoon
- 1 whisk
- 1 pastry brush
- 1 egg cutter
- 1 tin opener
- 1 bottle opener
- 1 lemon juice reamer
- 1 pepper mill
- 1 salt cellar

Soups

French Onion Soup
(serves 6)

	Peel, cut in half and thinly slice
500 g onions	Melt
50 g butter or margarine	in an uncovered pressure cooker and sweat the onion slices in it (photo 1)
	Pour on
1 l meat stock	Close the pressure cooker and bring to the boil. Add
125 ml (⅛ l) of white wine	to the soup. Season with
salt	
coarsely ground white pepper	Toast
2 slices of white bread	and cut into very small cubes
	Melt
30 g butter	and fry the bread cubes in it until they are crisp and brown (photo 2). Pour the onion soup into 6 bowls and sprinkle with the croutons. Sprinkle with
50 g Parmesan cheese	(photo 3) and gratinate under a hot grill. Serve immediately
Cooking time:	Roughly 4 minutes

P: 5 g, F: 15 g, Ch: 11 g, kJ: 933, kcal: 223.

Accompaniment: Small bread rolls.

Tip: It is worth preparing meat stock in advance and freezing it in 750 ml (¾ l) portions. In this way you will always be able to produce a vegetable or other soup in record time.

Soups

A good soup relies on a strong, tasty stock. Typical stock is made from bones, fish, beef, poultry, game or vegetables. These ingredients are covered with plenty of water, herbs and spices are added and the pot is left to simmer on low heat until a flavorsome liquid has been produced.

There are two types of stock:
1. Meat stock (low in fat)
2. Consommé (fat free and clarified, twice as strong as 1).

3. Consommé double (fat free and clarified, twice as strong as 2).

The stronger concentration of the stocks is achieved by:
- increasing the quantity of meat added,
- frying the ingredients before adding the water,
- frequent reducing (evaporation) of the stock.

Bone and meat stocks contain a large proportion of uric acid, a fact which should be taken into consideration when preparing a menu.

As opposed to stocks, **Cream soups** are always thickened, e.g. with flour, cornflour, kneaded butter, crème fraîche, puréed vegetables or potatoes, egg yolk or a mixture of egg yolk and cream.

To make a tasty stock, you need not only meat and bones but also soup vegetables or a bouquet garni and/or an onion stuck with cloves.

Soup vegetables
These include equal sized pieces of leek, celeriac, carrot and parsley root. This is normally available ready packed at your supermarket. 1 pack (about 200 g) is needed for 1 – 2 l of stock.

Onion stuck with cloves
Remove the outer skin from the onion but leave on the clean brown skin (this gives the stock a nice colour). Stick 1 – 2 cloves into the onion. The aroma this produces helps to balance the final flavour.

Bouquet garni
A bunch of herbs and soup vegetables. The following may be added to the soup vegetables: 1 – 2 twigs of thyme, 1 small twig of savory, 1 – 2 bay leaves, a sprig of parsley and a glove of garlic, if liked. The prepared, washed and tied bouquet garni is then placed into the stock and can easily be removed when the cooking time is over.

Making stock

1. Wash the ingredients carefully in cold water and place into the stock pot.

2. Add cold water to cover the ingredients, cover and bring to the boil.

3. Remove scum that has formed from congealed protein and cloudy matter.

4. The soup vegetables should be added after the liquid has been skimmed.

Note

If the ingredients are started in **cold** water, they lose more flavour, i.e. the full flavour goes into the stock. (This gives a very tasty meat stock.) If the meat is placed into **boiling** water, the pores are immediately sealed. This means that the meat will stay juicy and tender. (Extremely flavorful boiled beef.)

5. Turn down the heat and leave the ingredients to simmer gently for at least 1 hour.

6. If a very clear stock is required, the liquid can be poured through a sieve lined with a drying cloth.

Soups

Clarifying stock

There are various methods of doing this (see photos on the right).

1. Add 1–2 beaten egg whites to the stock. Bring to the boil, stirring continuously. The egg white will congeal around the cloudy matter. Strain the stock.

2. a) Finely chop 100 g of celeriac and carrots per litre of stock, sauté and leave to cool off.
   b) Beat 2–3 egg whites until stiff. Fold in the cooled vegetables.

Degreasing stock

1. For cooks in a **hurry**
   a) remove floating fat with a large, flat spoon.
   b) Draw strongly absorbent kitchen paper across the surface of the soup. It will absorb the fatty layer.
2. If you have **more time**, allow the stock to cool down. The fat will float to the surface and congeal. When the soup has cooled down fully the solid fat can be easily removed.

   Notes:
   – Do not salt the stock until you are ready to use it for a specific recipe. Salted stock becomes even saltier when it is reduced.
   – Do not cook pasta, rice or dumplings in clarified stock, as the stock will become cloudy. Cook the pasta, etc. separately and add it to the stock directly before serving.

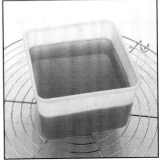

c) Add the egg white mixture to the lukewarm stock, bring to the boil over a high heat, stirring continuously. The cooked egg white surrounds the cloudy matter and swims on the surface.

d) Strain off the liquid. Your stock is ready to use or can be frozen in portions for later.

Soup garnishes

The soup garnishes and stock base (fish, meat, poultry, game or vegetable stock) must complement one another. Neutral ingredients, such as pasta, rice or leeks, go with all types of soup. However, very strongly flavoured garnishes do not (e.g. ham or liver dumplings do not harmonize with the flavour of fish stock but rather with a meat or vegetable stock).

Here are some examples of harmonious combinations:

Fish stock with pieces of fish (steamed or smoked), mussels, shrimps, croutons, quenelles, sautéd strips of leek, carrot, or celeriac, dock leaves, lemon balm, dill or tarragon.

Meat stock with greencorn or liver dumplings, cheese or ham dumplings, pancake strips, chopped herbs, julienne vegetables, ravioli, cooked egg garnish, sausage dumplings.

Vegetable stock with barley, rice, soup noodles, semolina dumplings, poached egg, mushroom garnish, choux pastry garnish, pulses/legumes.

Soup garnishes can be divided into 3 categories depending on the amount of preparation time they need:

1. **ready made**
   e.g. chopped herbs, egg yolk, diced tomato, grated cheese, pastry garnish, shrimps, prawns, diced ham.

2. **not much preparation**
   e.g. beaten egg, cooked pasta or rice, sautéd vegetables (thinly sliced leek), croutons, toasted almonds.

3. **take time**
   e.g. pancake strips, ravioli, dumplings (semolina, cheese, liver, fish, bone marrow dumplings), sautéd vegetables (julienne, cut into shapes), cheese or ham dumplings, egg garnish (photos 1 – 4).

Soups

Pea soup with semolina dumplings

	Wash and drain
375 g shelled peas	
(1 ¼ kg unshelled)	Peel and finely dice
2 medium sized onions	Melt
20 g margarine	Sweat the onions in it until they become translucent. Add the peas (reserve 3 tbs), sweat for a moment and add
750 ml (¾ l) meat stock	Season with
salt	
pepper	Bring to the boil, simmer for about 15 minutes, then pass through a sieve. Prepare the
semolina dumplings	Add them to the soup with the reserved peas and cook for about 10 minutes. Stir in
10 g butter	Add salt to taste and sprinkle with
chopped parsley	if liked
Cooking time:	Approx. 25 minutes

P: 8 g, F: 9 g, Ch: 18 g, kJ: 762, kcal: 182.

Goulash soup

	Peel and slice
200 g onions	Peel and finely chop
1 clove of garlic	Quarter, trim and deseed
2 large peppers	
(1 red, 1 green, 400 g)	removing the white inner walls. Wash the peppers and cut them into thin strips. Plunge
3 medium sized tomatoes	into boiling water (do not allow to boil on). Skin them, remove the core and quarter them. Wash
300 g beef	under cold running water. Dry and cut into small cubes. Heat
40 g vegetable fat	and fry the meat in it on all sides. Add the vegetables and allow to fry for a few moments. Add
3 slightly heaped tbs tomato purée	
salt	
pepper	
sweet paprika powder	
extra hot paprika powder	
½ tsp carraway	
dried marjoram	

1 l water and simmer for approx. 45 minutes. Thicken the soup with
brown thickener Season to taste with salt, pepper, paprika,
tabasco
Cooking time: Approx. 45 minutes

P: 16 g, F: 12 g, Ch: 15 g, kJ: 1031, kcal: 246.

Tip: Goulash soup can be prepared a day in advance. It should be thickened just before it is served.

Cream of asparagus soup

Wash and peel from the top down
250 g soup asparagus Make sure that all the skin and any fibrous parts are removed and that the tips are not damaged. Cut the asparagus into 3 cm pieces. Bring
500 ml (½ l) water containing
salt
1 tsp sugar
10 g butter to the boil. Add the asparagus cut-offs and skins.
Boil until tender. Strain the liquid through a sieve.
Add
250 ml (¼ l) milk (3.5 % fat) Add the asparagus pieces, bring to the boil, cook until tender and drain in a colander. Measure 500 ml (½ l) of the liquid.
Melt
20 g margarine and stir
15 g white flour into it over a low heat, stirring until it is pale golden in colour.
Add
500 ml (½ l) asparagus cooking liquid and whisk briskly, to ensure that no lumps form. Bring the soup to the boil, simmer for 5 minutes, season with salt to taste. Beat
1 egg yolk with
2 tbs double cream (30 % fat) Stir into the soup. Do not allow the soup to come to the boil again. Cut
50 g sliced boiled ham into strips and add to the soup with the asparagus pieces.
Sprinkle with
1 tbs chopped parsley.
Cooking time: Approx. 30 minutes

P: 7 g, F: 14 g, Ch: 8 g, kJ: 820, kcal: 196.

Soups

Chervil soup

	Trim, wash and chop
1 bunch soup vegetables	Melt
10 g margarine	Gently sauté the soup vegetables in the margarine. Peel, wash and dice
375 g potatoes	Wash
1 bunch chervil	under cold running water. Add with the sautéd soup vegetables to
750 ml (¾ l) meat stock	Season with
salt	Bring to the boil and simmer until tender. Pass the soup through a sieve. Add
125 ml (⅛ l) double cream (30 % fat)	Reheat the soup and add salt to taste. Stir in
2 tbs chopped chervil leaves	
Cooking time:	Approx. 20 minutes

P: 3 g, F: 12 g, Ch: 20 g, kJ: 883, kcal: 211.

Bone marrow dumplings

	Melt
40 g beef bone marrow	Pass it through a sieve and leave to cool. When cool, stir until smooth. Add
1 egg, 1 egg yolk, salt	
grated nutmeg, 50 g breadcrumbs	The mass must be smooth (see photo 1). Stir in
1 pinch baking powder	Leave the mixture to stand for 20 minutes. With wet hands, or two teaspoons, shape small dumplings (photo 2) and add these to boiling water or soup (photo 3). Simmer on very low heat until cooked (the liquid must move gently).
Cooking time:	Approx. 3 minutes

P: 4 g, F: 12 g, Ch: 11 g, kJ: 745, kcal: 178.

Soups

Beef Stock

Wash

250 g chopped beef bones
250 g shin of beef   under cold running water. Pat dry and put both ingredients into
1 ½ l cold salted water   Bring to the boil, remove scum, simmer gently.

Trim, wash and, if necessary, chop

1 bunch soup vegetables
2 medium sized onions   Add both these ingredients to the meat about 1 hour before the end of the cooking time. Cook until tender. Pass the liquid through a sieve, season to taste with salt. Cut the meat into cubes, add to the soup and sprinkle with

2 tbs chopped parsley
Cooking time: Approx. 2 ½ hours

P: 11 g, F: 12 g, Ch: 6 g, kJ: 787, kcal: 188.

Garnish: Egg garnish or bone marrow dumplings, rice or noodles.

Vegetable Stock

Trim, wash and chop

1 piece of celeriac
1 medium sized kohlrabi
1 medium sized carrot
1 medium sized onion
1 leek
100 g asparagus pieces   Melt
40 g butter or margarine   and use it to sauté the vegetables. Add
1 ¼ l hot water   Bring to the boil and cook the vegetables until tender. Shortly before the end of the cooking time wash and add
1 bunch parsley   Strain the liquid through a sieve and use instead of beef stock
Cooking time: Approx. 1 hour

P: 2 g, F: 9 g, Ch: 7 g, kJ: 490, kcal: 117.

Variations: Add parsley root, cauliflower stalks, white or savoy cabbage leaves.

Tip: Use frozen soup vegetables instead of fresh.

Chicken Stock
(serves 6)

	Wash
1 ready-to-use boiling fowl (1 kg)	under cold running water and put, with the heart, the split, cleaned stomach and gizzard, into a pan containing
1 ½ l boiling salted water	Bring almost to boiling point, skim off scum.
	Trim, wash and chop
1 bunch soup vegetables	then peel
1 medium sized onion	and add them to the liquid. Simmer the chicken until tender. Strain the stock through a sieve, season to taste with salt. Remove the meat from the bones, remove the skin and cut the meat into small pieces. Add
200 g cooked asparagus pieces	
125 g cooked long grain rice (parboiled)	to the stock. Reheat and sprinkle with
2 tbs chopped parsley	
Cooking time:	Approx. 1 ½ hours

P: 24 g, F: 25 g, Ch: 9 g, kJ: 1590, kcal: 380.

Egg Garnish

	Beat
2 eggs	with
125 ml (⅛ l) cold milk (3.5 % fat)	
salt	
grated nutmeg	Pour into a greased container, cover with aluminium foil and stand in boiling water. Bring the water back to the boil, cover the pan (the water must just be simmering now). When the mixture has set, turn it out of the container and cut it into cubes. Add to the soup
Cooking time:	Approx. 30 minutes

P: 4 g, F: 4 g, Ch: 2 g, kJ: 272, kcal: 65.

Variations:	Beat 1 tbs finely chopped herbs, finely grated cheese or tomato purée into the egg mixture
Tip:	Egg garnish is very easy to make in a microwave oven

Soups

Potato Soup

	Peel and dice
2 medium sized onions	Trim, wash and chop
1 bunch soup vegetables	Melt
15 g margarine	and sauté the chopped onion and soup vegetables in it.
	Peel, wash and dice
250 g potatoes	Add to the vegetables with
500 ml (½ l) instant stock (cube)	Bring to the boil, cook until tender, pass the soup through a sieve. Reheat and season with
salt	
pepper	
dried basil	Cut
1 bread roll	into cubes. Melt
15 g butter	Fry the cubed bread in the butter until brown.
	Serve the soup sprinkled with
2 tbs finely chopped chives and the croutons	
Cooking time:	Approx. 10 – 12 minutes

P: 3 g, F: 7 g, Ch: 21 g, kJ: 690, kcal: 165.

Variation: Add 2 skinned, diced tomatoes to the soup.

Clear Oxtail Soup
(Serves 6)

	Wash
750 g chopped oxtail	under cold running water, and pat dry. Dice
60 g smoked bacon	Heat
40 g vegetable fat	Fry the oxtail and bacon in the fat until browned all over. Trim, wash and chop
1 bunch soup vegetables	Add to the meat and heat through for a moment. Peel and cut in half
1 medium sized onion	Add to the meat together with
1 bay leaf, 2 cloves, 4 peppercorns, 2 allspice berries, (Jamaica pepper), salt	Pour on
1 l water	Cook until tender. Pour the liquid through a sieve and leave to cool. Remove fat from the surface. Cut the meat off the bones and dice. Add to the soup and season with salt
pepper	
sugar	

Stir
4 tbs sherry   into the soup and sprinkle with
2 tbs chopped parsley
Cooking time: Approx. 1 ½ hours

> P: 16 g, F: 18 g, Ch: 4 g, kJ: 1113, kcal: 266.

Semolina Dumplings

Bring
125 ml (⅛ l) milk (3.5 % fat)   to the boil with
10 g butter
salt
grated nutmeg   Remove from the heat. Stir in
50 g semolina   Continue stirring until you have a smooth ball. Stir for 1 more
minute. Put the hot mixture into a bowl and stir in
1 egg   Use two teaspoons to form small dumplings from the finished
mass. Add these to boiling salted water or soup and simmer until cooked (the liquid must move slightly)
Cooking time: Approx. 5 minutes

> P: 4 g, F: 5 g, Ch: 11 g, kJ: 452, kcal: 108.

Meat Dumplings

Beat
20 g butter or margarine   until soft. Add
50 g minced meat
1 egg yolk
salt
pepper
20 g breadcrumbs   Mix well. With damp hands shape small dumplings from the
mass, put them into boiling salted water or soup and simmer until cooked (the liquid must move slightly)
Cooking time: Approx. 5 minutes

> P: 4 g, F: 9 g, Ch: 4 g, kJ: 490, kcal: 117.

These dumplings are a very nice garnish for fricassee or stew.

Soups

Red Wine Soup

	Bring
375 ml (⅜ l) water	to the boil with
1 piece of cinnamon	
2 cloves	Peel, quarter, core and slice
1 small apple	Add to the water with
30 g sago	(photos 1 + 2). Stir, bring to the boil and cook until tender, stirring occasionally (remove the cinnamon and cloves). Add
375 ml (⅜ l) red wine	(photo 3). Reheat the soup but do not allow to boil. Add
75 g sugar	Add
lemon juice	to taste. Serve the soup hot or cold
Cooking time:	10 – 15 minutes

P: 0 g, F: 0 g, Ch: 30 g, kJ: 728, kcal: 174.

Garnish: Soup macaroons or toasted white bread cubes, pieces of apple or snow dumplings.

Snow Dumplings

	Stiffly beat
2 egg whites	Beat in
2 slightly rounded tsps sugar	Use a spoon to break off small dumplings and add these to boiling hot soup or water. Cover the pan and leave the dumplings to solidify (takes about 5 minutes)

P: 2 g, F: 0 g, Ch: 3 g, kJ: 75, kcal: 18.

Variations: Sprinkle the dumplings with grated chocolate or with sugar and cinnamon.

Soups

Porridge

	Sprinkle
40 g porridge oats	into
1 l boiling milk (3.5% fat)	Stir, bring to the boil and allow to swell. Add
50 g sugar	
1 pkt. vanilla-flavoured sugar	Season the porridge to taste with
salt	
grated lemon peel (untreated)	
Cooking time:	Approx. 10 minutes

P: 10 g, F: 10 g, Ch: 33 g, kJ: 1110, kcal: 263.

Variation: Stir 20 g butter into the porridge.

Bread Dumplings

	Melt
30 g butter	Stir in
1 beaten egg	
salt	
grated nutmeg	Add
50 g breadcrumbs	(enough to make a smooth mass). Add
1 pinch of baking powder	Stir into the mass and leave to stand for about 20 minutes. With damp hands shape dumplings, drop these into boiling salted water or boiling soup and simmer until cooked (the liquid must move slightly)
Cooking time:	Approx. 4 minutes

P: 3 g, F: 8 g, Ch: 11 g, kJ: 548, kcal: 131.

Tomato soup

	Place
500 g tomatoes	in boiling water (do not allow to boil on). Plunge them into cold water, peel, core and dice. Peel
2 medium sized onions	and dice along with
50 g fat bacon	Melt
20 g margarine	Sweat the diced onion and bacon in the margarine until the onion is translucent.

Add the diced tomato and sauté for a few minutes.
Dust with
20 g white flour Stir in
2 tbs tomato purée Add
750 ml (¾ l) instant stock (cube) Bring to the boil and boil for about 5 minutes. Press the soup through a sieve, reheat and season to taste with

salt, sugar
pepper (freshly ground)
paprika, sweet
chopped basil leaves
chopped thyme leaves
tabasco Sprinkle with
1 tbs chopped parsley Swirl in
1 pot (150 g) crème fraîche (30 % fat)

P: 4 g, F: 27 g, Ch: 12 g, kJ: 1356, kcal: 324.

Tip: Tinned tomatoes may be used instead of fresh ones.

Cold Sour Cherry Soup
(Serves 6)

Wash, drain, remove stalks and stones from
375 g sour cherries Add with
150 g sugar
1 piece lemon peel (untreated) to
500 ml (½ l) water and bring to the boil. Cook until almost tender.
Prepare
1 pkt. cherry-flavoured jelly as described on the packet. Add to the sour cherry soup and stir until fully dissolved. Refrigerate the soup for several hours before serving.

P: 2 g, F: 0 g, Ch: 34 g, kJ: 611, kcal: 146.

Sauces

Tomato Sauce

	Peel
1 small onion	and dice, along with
30 g smoked ham	Wash and chop
250 g tomatoes	Melt
20 g butter or margarine	Gently fry the diced ham in the fat, add the tomato and onion and sauté. Sprinkle with
20 g white flour	Heat through briefly and add
375 ml (⅜ l) water	Beat thoroughly with a whisk, ensuring no lumps form. Bring to the boil, and allow to boil for about 10 minutes. Pass through a sieve and season with
salt	
pepper	
lemon juice	
tomato purée	
Cooking time:	Approx. 10 minutes

P: 3 g, F: 7 g, Ch: 6 g, kJ: 427, kcal: 102.

Variation: Use tinned tomatoes (300 g) instead of fresh ones.
Make up the liquid from the tin to 375 ml (⅜ l) with water.

Tip: The tomato sauce is an ideal accompaniment to fish or pasta dishes.

Sauces

Preparing a good sauce is the height of culinary art, though it is not nearly as difficult as many housewives seem to think.
A dish itself quite often provides the base for a good sauce during the course of its preparation (e.g. chicken fricassee, marinated beef, goulash).

Many others, e.g. fried or grilled meat, do not produce any sauce or gravy base. In such cases we can use a previously frozen base or a convenience product.
The base for many sauces is a highly flavoured light or dark base (strong to very strong stock). It can be made from meat, poultry, game, fish or vegetables.

White base (stock). This is made by boiling fish heads and bones, or bones and meat, or a selection of soup vegetables in

water, spices and herbs for a long time (see also page 39, stocks).

When it has cooled off, the base gels and can be removed by the spoonful.

Dark base (gravy). Here it is important to ensure that the meat has been well browned. After it has been seasoned, and liquid (water, wine, stock) has been added, it must always be reduced and small quantities of liquid must be added to prevent

it burning. The more often this procedure is repeated, the stronger and better the gravy base will be. Any base which is not required immediately can be frozen in portions.

Sauces can be divided into the following categories:

- Basic white sauces (e.g. mushroom, bechamel, horseradish, cheese or caper sauce).
- Basic brown sauces (e.g. burgundy, pepper, or chasseur sauce).
- Emulsions (e.g. hollandaise, bearnaise or choron sauce).
- Gravies (unthickened).
- Cold sauces (e.g. on a quark, yoghurt, mayonnaise or cream base).

Thickening white and brown sauces

1. **Roux.** Sweat equal parts of flour and butter (e.g. 25 g flour and 25 g butter) over a low heat (allow to darken if you want a brown sauce). Stir continuously while slowly adding stock (base) until the desired consistency is achieved. This is mainly used for white sauces.

2. **Beurre Manie.** Fat (margarine, oil or butter) is kneaded with flour to make a paste. As much flour as possible should be worked into the fat. Small lumps of the mixture are added to the clear base, which is quickly

brought to the boil for a few moments, stirring continuously.

3. **Vegetables, onions.** Any vegetables that have been cooked in the liquid can be puréed or pressed through a sieve. This is a low calorie, easily digested thickener.

4. **Slaked flour, cornflour or starch.** The flour or starch is mixed or "slaked" with cold water in a separate bowl. It is then added to the hot liquid, stirring continuously, and simmered for a few moments. This method is not recommended from the point of view of flavour, as it can

easily mask the delicate aroma of fine sauces.

5. **Egg yolk, cream.** For white sauces, stir together egg yolk and a little cream. Slowly stir the mixture into the hot sauce base. Keep stirring strongly until the sauce has thickened. Do not allow to come to the boil.

6. **Double cream.** Reduce the base with sweet cream or crème fraîche until it has the

required consistency. Cream with a fat content of 10% is not suitable as it separates when heated.

7. **Yoghurt.** Beat yoghurt and stir into the sauce before it is served. Heat, stirring constantly, and do not allow to boil as the sauce will curdle.

8. **Pumpernickel, gingerbread.** Stir finely crumbled pumpernickel or gingerbread into dark sauces and cook for a while.

9. **Convenience products.** Stir in gravy thickeners or ready to use gravy powder as described on the packet.

Adapting sauces.

Basic white sauce e.g. with cheese, capers, chopped herbs, curry, lemon juice, white wine, horseradish, anchovy paste, tomato purée, julienne vegetables.

Basic brown sauces e.g. with fried diced onion, mushrooms, redcurrant jelly, cranberries, orange juice, crushed juniper berries, sour cherries, orange marmalade, crushed green peppercorns, red wine, sherry, brandy, mustard, crème fraîche.

Emulsions e.g. with chopped herbs, lemon juice, white wine, vegetable cooking liquor, crushed green peppercorns, paprika powder, grated cheese.

Sweet sauces e.g. with vanilla, ginger juice, orange juice, lemon juice, white wine.

Sauces

Emulsions

To make emulsion-based sauces it is very important to stick to a few basic rules to guarantee success.

1. Put all the ingredients for the sauce into a spotlessly clean pan, preferably with a rounded base.
2. Rule of thumb for light sauces: 1 egg yolk to 2 tbs water (wine, vegetable cooking liquor or fruit juice) or 1 tbs water and approx. 30 – 40 g melted butter or vegetable margarine (this is added drop by drop to the beaten egg). High fat sauces such as sauce hollandaise contain about 80 g of fat to 1 egg yolk.
3. For a water bath, fill the pan ¾ full with water, bring to a simmer (it must not boil).
4. Put ready all ingredients and utensils you will need for the sauce.
5. Put the vessel with the ingredients into the water bath or into a special, double walled

simmering pan. Beat the ingredients with a hand whisk or electric mixer until you have a smooth, foamy mixture.

6. If the sauce is prepared with melted fat, this must be clarified beforehand (skim off foam containing protein) and added to the foamy sauce, first drop by drop and then by the teaspoon, stirring continuously.

7. If you want to test the flavour of the sauce, use a clean spoon each time you dip into it.
8. Serve immediately.

Note:
If the sauce curdles, remove it from the water bath at once and stir in 1 – 2 ice cubes, a little lemon juice or 1 – 2 tbs cold cream.
Another possibility is to slowly stir the curdled sauce into 1 – 2 new egg yolks.

Mayonnaise-based sauces

Preparing mayonnaise.
1. Put all your ingredients and utensils ready.
2. Separate egg yolks and egg whites. The egg white can be frozen.
3. Mix together the egg yolks, seasoning and lemon juice or vinegar using a whisk. Stir until the mixture is homogeneous. Stir in one direction only.

4. Add oil, first drop by drop and then by the teaspoon, stirring continuously until the sauce is creamy.

White Sauce

Melt

25 g butter or margarine | Sweat
10 g white flour | in the fat, stirring continuously, until it is a pale golden colour. Add

250 ml (¼ l) milk (3.5 % fat)
125 ml (⅛l) double cream (30 % fat) | whisking the mixture briskly so that no lumps form. Bring to the boil and allow to boil gently for about 5 minutes. Beat together

1 egg yolk
2 tbs double cream (30 % fat) | Stir into the sauce, but do not allow the sauce to come to the boil again. Season to taste with

salt
lemon juice | Stir in
20 g butter
Cooking time: | Approx. 5 minutes

P: 4 g, F: 26 g, Ch: 5 g, kJ: 1172, kcal: 280.

Tip: The white sauce can be used as a basic sauce for fricassee and for boiled veal, fish or poultry.

Basic Brown Sauce

Melt

25 g margarine | Sweat
20 g white flour | in the fat until it is light to dark brown. Add
375 ml (⅜ l) instant stock (cube) | Beat well with a whisk, making sure no lumps form.
Bring to the boil and boil gently for about 5 minutes. Season to taste.
Cooking time: | Approx. 5 minutes

P: 1 g, F: 6 g, Ch: 4 g, kJ: 297, kcal: 71.

Tip: The basic brown sauce is a good base for chopped tongue or a Polish sauce which is delicious with carp.

Sauces

Sauce Béarnaise

	Melt
100 g butter	and leave to cool down a little. Peel and dice
1 small onion	and bring to the boil with
chopped tarragon leaves	
chopped basil leaves	
ground black pepper	
2 tsp wine vinegar	
2 tbs water	Allow to boil up for a moment before pouring through a sieve. Beat the liquid in a water bath together with
2 egg yolks	until the mixture thickens. Remove the bowl from the water bath, slowly beat in the slightly cooled butter and season the sauce with
salt	
pepper	
sugar	
lemon juice	Stir in
1 tbs chopped herbs	Keep the sauce warm in a water bath

P: 2 g, F: 24 g, Ch: 1 g, kJ: 987, kcal: 236.

Tip: Sauce béarnaise is ideal served with fine vegetables such as asparagus, broccoli or brussels sprouts, or with fried or grilled meat.

Sauces

Bacon Sauce

	Peel
1 medium sized onion	and dice, along with
50 g fatty bacon	Stir continuously over heat until they turn yellowish. Remove from the pan. Heat
20 g white flour	in the fat, stirring continuously until it turns brown. Add
375 ml (⅜ l) instant stock (cube)	Whisk thoroughly to ensure no lumps form. Stir in
½ bay leaf	
2 cloves	together with the diced onion and bacon, bring to the boil and cook for about 5 minutes. Add
2 tbs vinegar and season	with
salt	Remove the bay leaf and cloves before serving
Cooking time:	Approx. 5 minutes

P: 1 g, F: 11 g, Ch: 5 g, kJ: 565, kcal: 135.

Tip: Serve with French beans, potato dumplings, potatoes boiled in their skins or poached eggs.

Béchamel Sauce

	Peel
1 medium sized onion	and dice, along with
40 g smoked bacon	Melt
25 g butter or margarine	Fry the diced bacon in the fat until it crisps. Stir in
20 g white flour	together with the diced onion and stir over heat until the flour is pale yellow. Add
250 ml (¼ l) milk (3.5 % fat)	
125 ml (⅛ l) instant stock (cube)	Whisk thoroughly to ensure no lumps form. Bring to the boil and cook for about 10 minutes. Season with
salt, pepper	
Cooking time:	Approx. 10 minutes

P: 5 g, F: 11 g, Ch: 7 g, kJ: 636, kcal: 152.

Variation: Strain the sauce through a sieve.

Green Sauce

Wash and dry

1 bunch parsley
1 bunch chives
1 bunch chervil
1 bunch dill
1 bunch borage
1 bunch tarragon
1 bunch basil
½ box cress — Peel
1 small onion — Chop all the ingredients and put through the food processor for 1 – 2 minutes together with

1 pot (150 g) crème fraîche (30 % fat)
125 g quark (low fat) — Season the sauce to taste with
salt
pepper

P: 6 g, F: 12 g, Ch: 5 g, kJ: 649, kcal: 155.

Tip: Serve this sauce with salmon mousse, hard-boiled eggs or boiled beef.

Mustard Sauce

Melt

25 g butter or margarine — Stir in
10 g white flour — over a low heat until it turns pale yellow. Add
250 ml (¼ l) milk (3.5 % fat)
125 ml (⅛ l) double cream (30 % fat) — Whisk briskly, ensuring no lumps form. Bring to the boil and cook for about 5 minutes. Add
2 rounded tbs medium hot mustard — to the sauce, season with
salt
lemon juice
sugar
Cooking time: — Approx. 5 minutes

P: 5 g, F: 18 g, Ch: 5 g, kJ: 879, kcal: 210.

Sauce Remoulade

	Peel
2 hard-boiled eggs	Pass the yolks through a sieve and mix with
1 raw egg yolk	
salt	Drop by drop, and beating steadily, add half of
125 ml (⅛ l) salad oil	When the mixture is stiff enough add
2 tbs vinegar or lemon juice	
1 rounded tbs mustard	before adding the remaining oil. Finely chop
1 tbs capers	
1 medium sized gherkin	
2 tbs herbs (parsley, chives, dill, chervil, cress)	Add these ingredients to the mayonnaise and season with
pepper	
sugar	

P: 3 g, F: 34 g, Ch: 1 g, kJ: 1397, kcal: 334.

Variation: Chop the boiled egg white finely and add to the sauce.

Tip: Serve sauce remoulade with fried potatoes or cold meat.

Sauces

Sauce Hollandaise
(emulsion)

	Melt
200 g butter	Leave to cool off slightly. Beat together
2 egg yolks	
2 tbs white wine	in a water bath until the mixture thickens. Remove the bowl from the water bath and slowly beat in the cooled butter. Season the sauce with
lemon juice, salt, pepper	

P: 2 g, F: 45 g, Ch: 1 g, kJ: 1803, kcal: 431.

Crème Fraîche Sauce

	Mix together
1 pot (150 g) crème fraîche	
2 tbs milk (3.5 % fat)	
1 rounded tbs tomato ketchup	Season with
salt, pepper	Stir in
2 tbs chopped herbs (parsley, chives, dill, cress)	

P: 1 g, F: 12 g, Ch: 3 g, kJ: 531, kcal: 127.

Cumberland Sauce

	Remove the white part from the skin of
1 untreated orange	Cut the skin into fine strips and cook for about 10 minutes, until soft, in
3 tbs red wine	Mix together
250 g redcurrant jelly	
1 rounded tsp mustard	Add the red wine and cooled orange peel strips and season the sauce with
salt, lemon juice	

P: 0 g, F: 0 g, Ch: 40 g, kJ: 724, kcal: 173.

Tip: Serve with game, cold meat or pies.

Salad Dressing with Burnet

	Mix together
3 tbs salad oil	
3 tbs vinegar	
1 tsp medium hot mustard	
salt	
pepper	Stir
2 – 3 tbs finely chopped burnet leaves	into the dressing. Garnish with a few
burnet leaves	Salad dressing with burnet leaves is good with lettuce and webb lettuce

> P: 0 g, F: 11 g, Ch: 0 g, kJ: 418, kcal: 100.

Tip: This dressing can be stored in the refrigerator for several days.

Mayonnaise

	Put
1 egg yolk	
1 tbs vinegar or lemon juice	
salt	
sugar	into a mixing bowl and beat with a whisk or electric mixer until the mixture thickens. Beat in
125 ml (⅛ l) salad oil	(In this method it is not necessary to dribble in the oil, it can be added 1 – 2 tbs at a time. The seasoning that has been added to the egg yolk prevents the sauce from curdling). Season the mayonnaise with
mustard	if liked

> P: 1 g, F: 31 g, Ch: 1 g, kJ: 1226, kcal: 293.

Variation: If liked, yoghurt can be added to the sauce.

Tip: Curdled mayonnaise can be smoothed by beating in an extra egg yolk.

Fish

Plaice with Crispy Bacon

	Wash
4 cleaned and trimmed plaice (approx. 300 g each)	under running water and pat dry. Sprinkle with
lemon juice	Leave to stand for 30 minutes. Dry and sprinkle with
salt	
pepper	Turn in
white flour	(see photo 1). Heat
2 tbs cooking oil	in a large pan. Dice
20 g streaky bacon	and fry in the oil until crisp (photo 2). Remove the bacon from the pan and keep warm. Fry the plaice on both sides in the flavoured oil until brown (photo 3). Serve on a warm platter, sprinkle with the bacon and garnish with
wedges of lemon	
Frying time:	Approx. 15 minutes

P: 34 g, F: 34 g, Ch: 4 g, kJ: 2335, kcal: 558.

Accompaniments: boiled potatoes, lamb's lettuce.

Tip: To stop kitchen utensils and hands from smelling fishy, they should be rinsed in cold water before starting to prepare the fish.

69

Fish

Generally speaking, fish are high in protein, low in fat, and contain a high proportion of essential vitamins, trace elements and minerals. If properly prepared nearly all fish are easily digestible.

Fish are divided into two categories, see photos on right. There is usually more sea fish on offer than freshwater fish. Seafish are gutted on the trawler straight after they are caught and large fish may be divided up. The fish are cooled on ice (**not** frozen) and are put on the market as soon as the trawlers reach land. Freshwater fish are often kept alive and fresh in small aquariums. Fresh fish can be recognized by:

1. clear eyes;
2. red gills with no slime (lift the gills slightly and look underneath);
3. firm scales;
4. fresh, not unpleasant smell;
5. shiny bright skin covered with a clear slippery layer (colour changes to blue when boiled);
6. smooth shiny appearance of cut pieces.

1. Sea fish

These live in salt water. Examples are ocean perch, cod, haddock, halibut (1), plaice (1), Dover sole (1), eel (2), mackerel (2), herring (2).

2. Freshwater fish

These live in fresh water (lakes and rivers). Examples are pike (3), salmon trout (3), carp (3), brown trout (3), whitefish, pike-perch, tench, catfish.

Removing scales

1. Hold the tail firmly (if necessary with a cloth).
2. Using a fish scaler or a flat, wide-bladed knife, scrape off the scales from tail to head.

Tip:
The scales will fly around less if they are removed under running water.

3. **Carefully** remove the gut, taking care not to damage the gall bladder as this can make the fish inedible.
4. Wash away any blood under cold running water.
5. Continue as indicated in your recipe.

Skinning fish

1. Cut across the skin at the tail with a sharp knife.
2. Take hold of the tail with a cloth, see below.
3. Pull off the skin in the direction of the head with a short jerk.

Gutting fish

1. Take hold of the fish with your left hand.
2. Using a sharp knife carefully slit the belly of the fish from the tail to the gills.

Filleting fish

Example: Dover sole

1. Using a sharp knife cut along the backbone of the skinned fish, from tail to head.

2. Carefully separate the fillets from the bones. When both fillets have been removed from one side, turn the fish over and repeat the procedure on the other.

Fish

A fishy smell is avoidable.

Here are a few simple but effective tips:
1. Wrap the fish in a cloth soaked in vinegar.
2. When prepared, sprinkle with lemon juice and, if liked, with herbs. Cover and store in a cool place until needed.
3. Rub hands and any utensils that have been in contact with the fish with **cold** water or, better still, with vinegar or lemon juice.
4. Used crockery should **first** be rinsed under cold water before being washed in hot water and detergent.

Shellfish/Oysters

Generally speaking these live in salt water. Their laterally compressed bodies are contained by a shell which opens into 2 halves. They have delicate flesh which is high in protein and deteriorates quickly. This is why they are mainly available in the cooler seasons (months with an "R" in them).
There are many types of shellfish, e.g. scallops, clams, cockles, and various types of mussels.

The 123 method

1. Clean fish by holding it under cold running water for a moment and then patting dry. It is important not to damage the mucous layer on whole fish that are to be cooked in stock.

2. Always sprinkle fish with lemon juice, vinegar or white wine unless the fish is to be cooked in stock.

3. Salt the fish directly before it is cooked. Salt draws out water and fish will be dry if salted too far in advance. When marinating fish, use no salt in the marinade.

The following cooking methods are suitable for fish:
cooking in stock, stewing, steaming, frying, baking, smoking.

Fish is cooked when:
1. the fins and bones come away easily,
2. the skin comes away from the flesh easily,
3. the fish comes away in a scale pattern when pressed with a fork,
4. the eyes have come forward and are opaque.

Buying and preparing shellfish

1. Only buy shellfish if their shells are firmly shut. Any raw shellfish whose shells have opened slightly should be discarded as they could be bad.
2. With a sharp knife or scissors, remove any fibres or seaweed from shellfish.
3. Scrub thoroughly with a brush under cold running water.

Note:
Shellfish shells must open during cooking! Any which stay shut are bad and therefore inedible.

Crustaceans

Crustaceans are water dwellers. They have an outer calcified shell which can vary in thickness. These creatures can only grow if they regularly cast off their shells. They breathe through gills.
The shells contain a brownish black chromoprotein (protein compound with colourant), one of whose constituents is the red pigment astaxanthin. This is what causes the shells to turn red when the brownish black creatures are boiled.

1. Long tailed crustaceans: lobster, langoustine, crayfish.

2. Short tailed crustaceans: deep sea prawns, giant prawns, scampi tails, North Sea shrimps.

Shelling cooked prawns and shrimps

1. Take hold of the prawn or shrimp with one hand behind its head and one hand on the tail.
2. Twist the head and tail in opposite directions.
3. Lightly press the shell against the body and remove the meat.
4. Using a knife or skewer remove the intestinal tract which runs along the back.

Fish

Deep fried fish

	Wash
750 g fish fillets	
(cod, haddock, coley)	under cold running water and pat dry (photo 1). Sprinkle with
lemon juice or vinegar	and leave to stand for about 30 minutes. Pat dry, sprinkle with
salt, pepper	Cut into portions. For the batter, sieve
100 g white flour	into a bowl, make a depression in the centre. Beat together
1 egg	with
salt	
125 ml (⅛ l) milk	and pour some of this mixture into the depression. Mix together, starting in the centre and gradually adding the remaining egg and milk mixture. Add
1 tbs cooking oil	
or melted butter	ensuring that no lumps form. With a fork, dip the pieces of fish into the batter (photo 2) and fry them in deep, hot
fat (cooking oil,	
lard or coconut fat)	until brown and crisp. Drain on kitchen paper (photo 3).
Frying time:	Approx. 10 minutes

P: 39 g, F: 17 g, Ch: 20 g, kJ: 1715, kcal: 410.

Accompaniments: Potato salad.

Fish

Pickled fried herrings

	Gut and cut the heads off
4 medium sized fresh herrings (250 g each)	Wash under cold running water, remove scales and pat dry. Mix together
20 g white flour	
salt	Turn the herrings in the mixture. Heat
6 tbs cooking oil	in a frying pan and fry the herrings in it until brown on both sides. Peel and slice
2 medium sized onions	and put them with the herrings,
1 tbs mustard grains	
8 peppercorns	
a few allspice berries (Jamaica pepper)	in an earthenware pot. Mix together
250 ml (¼ l) vinegar	
125 ml (⅛ l) water	and pour over the herrings. The herrings are ready to eat after 4–6 days.
Frying time:	6–8 minutes

> P: 33 g, F: 47 g, Ch: 5 g, kJ: 2548, kcal: 609.

Tip: When frying whole fish it is important to ensure that all of the fish is in contact with the base of the frying pan, otherwise it will not cook evenly.

Mackerel in cheese sauce

	Wash
4 ready to use mackerel (250 g each)	under cold running water. Bring
500 ml (½ l) water	to the boil with
1 medium sized bay leaf	
juniper berries	
a few mustard grains	
1 rounded tsp salt	
1 pinch pepper	
4 tbs vinegar	Put the fish into the boiling liquid, bring to the boil again, reduce heat and simmer until cooked. Put the fish on a warmed plate and keep hot. For the cheese sauce strain the cooking liquor through a sieve and measure off 250 ml (⅛ l). Melt

25 g margarine Heat
10 g white flour in the margarine until it turns pale yellow. Add the fish stock and beat thoroughly with a whisk, making sure no lumps form. Bring the sauce to the boil and cook for about 5 minutes. Stir in

75 g grated Swiss cheese
4 tbs double cream Season with
salt
pepper
sugar Serve the mackerel with sauce poured over them or serve the sauce separately
Cooking time, fish: Approx. 10 minutes
Cooking time, sauce: Approx. 5 minutes

P: 36 g, F: 34 g, Ch: 2 g, kJ: 2075, kcal: 496.

Cod fillets with savoury topping

Wash
750 g cod fillets under cold running water, pat dry, and sprinkle with
2 tbs lemon juice Leave to stand for approx. 15 minutes. Pat dry again and place in a buttered baking dish. For the topping, beat

50 g butter or margarine until soft, and stir in
50 g breadcrumbs Peel and finely dice
1 medium sized onion
1 tbs chopped parsley
1 tbs finely chopped chives
1 level tsp sweet paprika powder
125 ml (⅛ l) white wine Season the topping with
salt
pepper
nutmeg Spread over the fish. Place the baking dish in the pre-heated oven
Electricity: 200 – 225
Gas: 6-7
Cooking time: 30 – 35 minutes

P: 35 g, F: 11 g, Ch: 13 g, kJ: 1385, kcal: 331.

Accompaniments: Green salad, French bread.

Fish

Fried Dover Sole

	Wash
4 ready to use Dover soles (300 g each)	under cold running water, pat dry and sprinkle with
4 tbs lemon juice	Sprinkle inside and out with
salt	Turn in
white flour	Heat
125 g herb-flavoured butter	Fry the soles in it on both sides, remove from pan, put on a warmed plate and keep warm. Clean, wash and slice
250 g mushrooms	Heat
50 g herb-flavoured butter	Sauté the mushrooms in the butter for about 10 minutes. Add
125 ml (⅛ l) white wine	
125 ml (⅛ l) double cream	Stir well, bring to the boil, remove from heat. Beat
2 egg yolks	Stir into the sauce, season with salt, pepper, and pour over the soles. Heat
25 g herb-flavoured butter	Fry
50 g chopped almonds	in the butter, sprinkle over the fish.
Frying time:	Approx. 6 minutes each side

> P: 44 g, F: 65 g, Ch: 10 g, kJ: 3577, kcal: 855.

Accompaniments: Rice, green salads or small potatoes cooked with herbs, chicory salad.

Tip: The dark skin is always removed from Dover sole whether it is cooked whole or as fillets. (See Essential Information for information on filleting)

Dover sole rolls in cream sauce

	Wash
8 Dover sole fillets (600 g)	under running cold water, pat dry, and sprinkle with
2 tbs lemon juice	Leave to stand for 15 minutes, pat dry again, sprinkle with
salt	Finely chop
115 g sautéd mushrooms	Mix together with
2 tbs chopped parsley	
1 tbs chopped dill	Divide the mixture among the fillets, roll them up and secure with skewers

For the cream sauce
boil

250 ml (¼) double cream (30 % fat) until reduced by half, season with
salt
curry powder Simmer the fish rolls in the sauce until cooked, then remove and serve on a warmed plate. Season the sauce with salt and pour over the fish.

Cooking time: Approx. 10 minutes

P: 29 g, F: 22 g, Ch: 1 g, kJ: 1431, kcal: 324.

Accompaniments: Boiled potatoes sprinkled with parsley.

Fishcakes

Peel and slice
1 large onion Heat
2 tbs olive oil in a frying pan, add the onion slices, season with
salt Sauté for about 10 minutes until cooked, remove from the pan. Add
1 tbs olive oil to the pan. Prepare
1 pack (250 g) frozen fish cakes as described on the package. Reserve on a warmed plate. Return the sliced onion to the pan. Add
3 tbs evaporated milk (7.5 % fat)
2 level tsp grated horseradish (jar) Heat through and pour over the fishcakes.

Cooking time: 15 – 20 minutes

P: 10 g, F: 12 g, Ch: 5 g, kJ: 887, kcal: 212.

Fish

Fried fillets of pike

	Wash
4 pike fillets	under cold running water, pat dry, sprinkle with
lemon juice	Leave to stand for 30 minutes. Pat dry again, sprinkle with
salt	Dice
50 g fatty bacon	Fry until crisp in
1 tbs cooking oil	Fry the fillets in the oil until brown on both sides. Serve on a warmed plate. Garnish with
parsley	
Cooking time:	Approx. 10 minutes

P: 28 g, F: 19 g, Ch: 0 g, kJ: 1305, kcal: 312.

Poached Coalfish

	Wash
750 g coalfish fillet	under cold running water, pat dry, sprinkle with
2 tbs lemon juice	Leave to stand for 15 minutes, pat dry again, sprinkle with
salt	
pepper	Peel and dice
1 small onion	Melt
20 g butter or margarine	Sauté the onion in the butter until translucent, then add fish fillet,
2 tbs water	
10 peppercorns	
1 small bay leaf	
1 clove	
2 allspice berries (Jamaica pepper)	When cooked serve the fish on a warmed plate and garnish with
lemon slices	
parsley	
Cooking time:	8 – 10 minutes

P: 34 g, F: 6 g, Ch: 1 g, kJ: 862, kcal: 206.

Accompaniments:	Boiled potatoes, mixed salad.
Variations:	Instead of using coalfish, use cod, ocean perch, halibut (cooking time: 8 – 10 minutes) or leng (cooking time: 10 – 12 minutes).

Poached carp "blue"

	Wash
1 ready to use carp	under cold running water. Rub the inside with salt. (Do not rub salt on the outside as this would damage the mucous layer which gives the fish its blue colour when cooked.) Peel and dice
1 medium sized onion	Melt
30 g butter or margarine	Sauté the onion in the butter until translucent, then add fish,
5 tbs water	
20 peppercorns	
1 bay leaf	
1 clove	
3 allspice berries	Poach until cooked. Serve the fish on a warmed plate
Cooking time:	40–45 minutes

P: 30 g, F: 14 g, Ch: 1 g, kJ: 1105, kcal: 264.

Accompaniments:	Boiled potatoes flavoured with herbs, melted butter.
Variations:	Instead of using carp the following fish may be used: 1. Trout, 300 g each, tied into a round – poaching time: 20-25 minutes. 2. Tench, 300 g each, tied into a round, poaching time: 25 – 30 minutes.

Salted herrings housewife-style

	Thoroughly water
6 salted herring fillets	for 1–2 hours, then drain well, cut into 2 cm pieces.
	For the cream sauce
	peel and slice
200 g onions	and slice
2 gherkins	Mix together
375 ml (⅜ l) double cream	
4–5 tbs vinegar	
1 tbs mustard seeds	
8 peppercorns	Add the sliced onion and gherkins. Put the herring into the sauce and leave to stand for 24 hours
Variation:	Peel, quarter, core and slice 2 apples and add to the sauce

P: 23 g, F: 58 g, Ch: 8 g, kJ: 2841, kcal: 679.

Accompaniment:	Potatoes boiled in their skins, green beans and bacon bits or fried potatoes.

Eel in cream and cress sauce

	Prepare
1 fresh eel (about 1 kg)	Take hold of the fish with a kitchen towel. With a sharp, pointed knife make a cut about 2 cm long just under the head on the underside of the eel. Make cuts in the skin all round the body. Hold the head firmly in the kitchen towel, loosen the skin under the head (see photo 1) and jerk off the skin, pulling towards the tail (photo 2). Cut off the head. Take hold of the body of the eel and, using a 2 pronged meat fork, remove the intestines from the body cavity with a twisting movement (photo 3). Rinse the fish under cold running water, pat dry, and cut into pieces about 7 cm long. Bring to the boil
about 1 ½ l water	containing
salt and vinegar	Peel
1 onion	Stick it with
2 cloves	and add to the water with
1 bay leaf	Add the fish, bring to the boil and simmer until cooked. Remove from the liquid, drain and keep warm. For the cream and cress sauce peel and finely dice
2 shallots	Melt
100 g butter	Sauté the shallots in the butter until translucent. Add
100 ml instant meat stock (cube)	
100 ml white wine	Stir in
300 ml double cream	Reduce the liquid until it has a creamy consistency. Wash the leaves from
1 box cress	under cold running water and stir into the sauce with
2 tbs crème fraîche	Season the sauce with
salt, pepper	Return the eel to the sauce to heat through
Cooking time for the eel:	Approx. 15 minutes

P: 29 g, F: 92 g, Ch: 4 g, kJ: 4284, kcal: 1024.

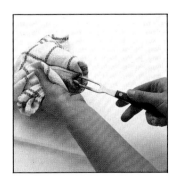

Fish

Stuffed coalfish fillet

Wash

750 g coalfish fillet under cold running water, pat dry and sprinkle with

2 tbs lemon juice Leave to stand for 15 minutes. For the stuffing, prepare

1 pack (300 g) frozen spinach as described on the package. Dry the fish again and sprinkle with

salt

pepper Line a baking tin with half of the fish.
Distribute the stuffing over the fish, cover with the remaining fish. For the topping, mix together

1 pot (150 g) crème fraîche (30 % fat)

salt

10 g grated parmesan cheese Spread the mixture over the fish. Put the fish into the preheated oven

Electricity: 200 – 225

Gas: 6-7

Cooking time: 35 – 40 minutes

P: 38 g, F: 14 g, Ch: 3 g, kJ: 1284, kcal: 307.

Steamed cod

Wash

1 ¼ kg ready to use cod (in one or more pieces) under cold running water, pat dry and sprinkle with

2 tbs lemon juice Leave to stand for 15 minutes. Put

250 ml (¼ l) water

1 pkt. (75 g) frozen soup herbs

1 bay leaf

10 peppercorns

3 cloves

5 allspice berries

1 peeled, diced onion

1 tsp salt

1 tbs vinegar into a fish kettle. Place the fish on the platform, bring the liquid to the boil and cook the fish in the steam. When ready serve on a heated plate.

Cooking time: Approx. 20 minutes
Accompaniments: Melted butter, boiled potatoes
Variations: The following fish can be used instead of cod:
1. Haddock, steaming time approx. 20 minutes
2. Coalfish, steaming time approx. 20 minutes
3. Ocean perch, steaming time approx. 20 minutes
4. Leng, steaming time approx. 30 minutes
5. Pike-perch (descaled, gutted, without fins, with head), steaming time approx. 30 minutes
6. Pike (descaled, gutted, without fins, with head), steaming time approx. 30 minutes
7. Eel – ½ recipe – (gutted, skinned, without head, cut into 5 cm portions), steaming time approx. 20 minutes

P: 42 g, F: 1 g, Ch: 2 g, kJ: 858, kcal: 205.

Cod baked in the oven

	Wash
1 ¼ kg oven-ready cod (in one or more pieces)	under cold running water, pat dry and sprinkle with
2 tbs lemon juice	Dry the fish again, and rub inside and out with
salt	
pepper	Leave to stand for 15 minutes. Put the fish into a buttered baking dish, cover with
50 g fatty bacon slices	and bake in the preheated oven
Electricity:	175–200, Gas: 3-4
Cooking time:	Approx. 40–45 minutes

P: 42 g, F: 11 g, Ch: 0 g, kJ: 1259, kcal: 301.

Variations: The following fish can be used instead of cod:
1. Haddock, cooking time 40–45 minutes
2. Coalfish, cooking time 40–45 minutes
3. Ocean perch, cooking time 40–45 minutes
4. Leng, cooking time 40–45 minutes
5. Pike-perch (descaled, gutted, without fins, with head), cooking time 45–50 minutes
6. Pike (descaled, gutted, without fins, with head), cooking time 45–50 minutes
7. Eel (gutted, skinned, without head, cut into 5 cm portions), cooking time 25–30 minutes

Fish

Grilled fillets of plaice in almond butter

	Wash
8 fillets of plaice (600 g)	under cold running water, pat dry and sprinkle with
salt	Put the fillets on to 2 large pieces of aluminium foil, 4 on each piece (photo 1).
	For the almond butter mix together
50 g butter	
40 g peeled almonds	
ground almonds	
salt	(photo 2). Spread this over the fillets (photo 3) and push the fillets under the hot grill, still on the foil.
Grilling time:	
Electricity:	Approx. 15 minutes
Gas:	Approx. 15 minutes

P: 28 g, F: 17 g, Ch: 2 g, kJ: 1201, kcal: 287.

Accompaniment: Potato salad.

Tip: Fresh fish can be kept in the refrigerator, wrapped loosely in aluminium foil or cling film until it is prepared.

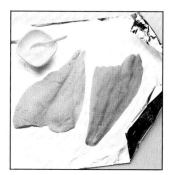  

Fish

Fried fresh herrings

	Wash
1 ¼ kg ready to use fresh herrings	under cold running water, pat dry. Mix together
2 tbs white flour	
salt	
pepper	Turn the herrings in this mixture. Heat
5 tbs cooking oil	Fry the herrings on both sides
Cooking time:	6–8 minutes

> P: 40 g, F: 50 g, Ch: 4 g, kJ: 2782, kcal: 665.

Accompaniments: Fried potatoes, potato salad or potatoes boiled in their skins.

Trout with almonds

	Wash
4 ready to use trout (200 g each)	under cold running water, pat dry and sprinkle with
2 tbs lemon juice	Leave to stand for 15 minutes, pat dry again and rub the trout inside and out with
salt	Turn the fish in
20 g white flour	(photo 1). Heat
50 g margarine	in a frying pan and fry the trout on both sides until brown (photo 2). About 5 minutes before the end of the cooking time, add
100 g peeled, split almonds	to the frying pan (photo 3) and brown.
Cooking time:	Approx. 10 minutes

> P: 25 g, F: 27 g, Ch: 8 g, kJ: 1643, kcal: 393.

Accompaniments: Boiled potatoes sprinkled with parsley, green salad.

Fish

Fried ocean perch fillet

	Wash
750 g ocean perch fillet	under cold running water, pat dry, cut into portions and sprinkle with
2 tbs lemon juice	Leave to stand for 30 minutes, pat dry, sprinkle with
salt	
pepper	Mix together
1 egg	
2 tbs cold water	Turn the fillets first in
white flour	then in the beaten egg and finally in
75 g breadcrumbs	Heat
80 g margarine	Fry the fish fillets in the margarine until browned on both sides.
Cooking time:	10 – 12 minutes

> P: 38 g, F: 24 g, Ch: 20 g, kJ: 2021, kcal: 483.

Variation: Use coalfish, leng, cod or fillets of sole instead of ocean perch (cooking time: approx. 15 minutes).

Halibut in lemon and dill sauce

	Wash
1 kg ready to use halibut	under cold running water, pat dry, and sprinkle with
2 tbs lemon juice	Leave to stand for 15 minutes, pat dry, rub inside and out with
salt	Put
1 pkt frozen soup herbs	
125 ml (⅛ l) white wine	into a large pan, lay the fish on top and push into the preheated oven (the fish is cooked when the dorsal fin comes away easily from the flesh). Serve the cooked halibut on a warmed plate and pour on
40 g melted butter	Garnish with
lemon wedges	
tomato wedges	
parsley	For the lemon and dill sauce, mix together
1 pot (150 g) crème fraîche (30 % fat)	
5 tbs milk (3.5 % fat)	
2 tbs lemon juice	

1 tsp grated lemon peel (jar)
2 tbs chopped dill Season to taste with
salt, sugar
Electricity: 175 – 200
Gas: 3-4
Cooking time: Approx. 30 minutes

P: 43 g, F: 66 g, Ch: 5 g, kJ: 1908, kcal: 456.

Accompaniment: Boiled potatoes flavoured with herbs, green salad.

Cod in garlic sauce

Take
1 pkt (400 g) frozen cod fillets from the package, thaw for 10 minutes, sprinkle with
2 tbs lemon juice Leave to stand for 15 minutes. Put into a buttered baking dish.

For the garlic sauce
peel and finely dice
3 cloves of garlic
1 medium sized onion Heat
3 tbs olive oil Sweat the garlic and onion in the hot oil. Plunge
350 g firm tomatoes into boiling water (do not allow to boil again), refresh them in
cold water, remove the skins and cores and dice the flesh. Add
to the other ingredients together with

2 tbs chopped parsley
1 tbs dried oregano Season the sauce with
salt, sugar Pour over the fish. Put the baking dish into the pre-heated oven
Electricity: 200 – 225
Gas: 5-6
Cooking time: Approx. 25 – 30 minutes

P: 18 g, F: 11 g, Ch: 4 g, kJ: 791, kcal: 189.

Accompaniment: Boiled potatoes

Meat

Boiled Ox Tongue
(serves 6)

	Wash
1kg ready to use, salted ox tongue	under cold running water. Peel
2 medium sized onions	Spike with
4 cloves	and put into
1 l boiling salted water	with
1 bay leaf	
1 pkt. frozen soup vegetables	Cook the tongue until tender (test by pricking the tip, which should be soft) (photo 1).
	Wash off the cooked tongue with cold water, remove the skin (photo 2), and remove the tough cartilage from the end while the tongue is still hot.
	Return the tongue to the hot liquid until you are ready to serve it. When ready, cut it into finger thick slices (photo 3) and serve on a warmed plate
Cooking time:	Approx. 2 hours

P: 27 g, F: 27 g, Ch: 2 g, kJ: 1598, kcal: 382.

The calculation includes the liquid.

Accompaniments: Peas, carrots and cauliflower, horseradish sauce, boiled potatoes.

Tip: The tongue can also be eaten cold with horseradish or herb sauce and French bread.

Meat

Preparation and storage

Meat should be used as fresh as possible. Wash whole pieces of meat under cold running water and pat dry. Cover and store in an earthenware container in the refrigerator until you are ready to use it. If meat is not required for immediate use, it can be appropriately packaged and fast frozen.

Tip:
Brush small pieces of prepared meat with oil and refrigerate them. This stops them from drying out and makes them more tender.

Cooking methods

Boiling = cooking in a large quantity of simmering liquid.

1. Lower the meat into the **simmering** liquid. It will stay juicy and tender.
2. The liquid (water, possibly mixed with vinegar or wine)

should cover the meat **completely**.

3. The heat should be adjusted so that the liquid simmers continuously.

Note:
If you wish to remove the fat from the liquid, allow it to cool off. The fat will then solidify and can easily be lifted off. Any left over liquid can be cooled and frozen.

Pot roasting = cooking by frying quickly in hot fat, then continuing to cook in simmering liquid and steam.

1. Fry the dried meat in **hot** fat.
2. Add the onions and fry.

3. Add a little hot liquid.
4. Turn down heat, cover pan and leave to cook. The level of the liquid should not rise above ¼ of the height of the meat.
5. Keep replacing liquid which has been reduced.

Note: Pot roasted dishes can also be cooked in the oven in a pan with a tight fitting lid.

Carving meat

1. Before starting to carve, wrap meat in aluminium foil and leave for about 10 minutes to rest. This permits the meat juices to spread through the meat and stops them from running out when the meat is cut.
2. Always cut meat across the grain of the fibre.

Frying = cooking and browning in a little fat.

The meat can be plain, flour coated or breadcrumbed before frying.

1. Lower the dried meat into **hot** fat. This seals the pores quickly and the meat stays juicy.
2. Fry until crisply cooked on setting 1½ – 2 (automatic burner 6 – 7).
3. Turn the meat when it comes away easily from the bottom of the pan.

Note:
Since onions draw water, they should be added after the meat has browned sufficiently.
To make gravy, add a little liquid (water, stock, cream, etc.) and boil off the pan juices.

Roasting = cooking and browning with or without the addition of fat in an open container in the oven.

1. Set the oven to the required temperature.
2. Pour a little water into the bottom of the roasting pan.
3. Place the prepared, seasoned meat on the wire rack or into the roasting pan.
4. Add liquid (preferably hot) when the pan juices start to brown and the existing liquid has been reduced through evaporation.

Note:
The roasting temperature may be kept constant or you can start to roast on a high temperature and reduce the heat later (e.g. from 200° to 175° degrees C).
Oven bricks are suitable for roasting in. Always remember to **water** them before putting them into the cold oven. A crisp roast can also be prepared in a roasting bag.

Coating = covering meat with a coating to prevent it from drying out.

Turn the dried meat
1. in flour
2. in beaten egg and breadcrumbs.

Note:
Cook coated meat immediately to stop the coating from becoming soggy. Breadcrumbs can be replaced with grated cheese, desiccated coconut, crumbled rusks, chopped nuts or almonds, sesame seeds or ground sunflower seeds.

Is it cooked?

Press the meat with a spoon to see how far it has cooked:

soft = roast is red inside
springy = roast is pink inside (can be pressed down)
firm = roast cooked through (cannot be pressed down)

Meat

Beef

Beef is divided into the following categories, depending on the age of the animal from which it comes.

Young beef (animals up to 1 year old)

Beef from young bulls (animals up to 2 years old)

Meat from heifers, oxen, very young cows (animals up to about 5 years)

Meat from young cows (animals up to about 5 years)

Cow meat (animals older than 5 years)

Beef from **young animals** is a bright light to brick red colour with white to pale yellow fat marbling. Its cut surface is shiny and the texture of the meat is fine to medium fine.

Beef from **older animals** has a darker reddish brown colour with yellowish fat marbling and a coarser texture.

Beef must be well hung before being used. This makes it soft and tender and is known as maturing.

Hanging time:

for boiling	3-5 days
for roasting	5-8 days
for frying	approx. 8 days

Tip: raw meat can be tenderized by freezing it.

For **roasting**: use rump, fillet, rib, topside, silverside, aitchbone.

For **pot roasting**: use topside, aitchbone, flank, top rump, bladebone.

For **frying and grilling**: use slices of rump, fillet, chateaubriand, sirloin, topside, silverside, liver.

For **boiling**: use neck, top rib, clod, breast, top rib, brisket, topside, flank, skirt, shin, tail, lungs, heart, tongue, kidneys.

Cuts of beef

Top rib, neck. Muscle marbled with fat, strongly grained.

Sticking piece. Lower side of the neck.

Top rib, fore rib. Tender steaks are cut from the centre.

Sirloin, from the middle of the back. Cuts into sirloin and rump steaks.

Brisket. The cut located between the two front legs.

Thin flank contains fat and sinew.

Fillet. Most valuable cut; for steaks.

Rump and aitchbone. Lean cuts from the back, towards the tail. More expensive cuts.

Lean rump, small cut from the hind quarter.

Meat

Cuts of beef

Topside, very tender cut from the leg. Expensive cut.

Silverside, lean cut from the leg, finely marbled with fat.

Flank, a cut from the mid to hindquarters.

Shin, slice through the lower leg. Lean, with lots of connective tissue. Bone contains marrow with high fat content.

Chuck, tender cut from the forequarter.

Bladebone, tender cut from the forequarter. Slightly coarse texture.

Veal

Veal comes from young calves between 4 and 10 weeks old. Under no circumstances may they be older than 3 months. Veal is finely textured, pale red (contains iron) and is lean or low in fat.

For **roasting**: use leg, loin, sirloin, fillet, breast, knuckle. The following cuts are suitable for **braising**: neck, breast, shoulder, knuckle.

For **grilling and frying**: use slices of loin and leg, sirloin, knuckle, chops, fillet, liver, brains, sweetbread, kidney. The following cuts are suitable for **boiling**: scrag, breast, knuckle, flank, liver, heart, sweetbread, brains.

Cuts of veal

Best end of neck. Tender, short fibred cut, usually sold on the bone.

Middle neck, loin. The fillet is removed and sold separately.

Breast. Very meaty cut from fattened calves.

Leg. Prime cut, usually roasted. Can be sliced for veal cutlets.

Cut from the leg. Prime roasting meat, ideal for schnitzels.

Knuckle, end of leg. Contains lean muscle and sinews.

Meat

Pork

Generally speaking, the pork sold at the butcher shop comes from animals **under** 1 year old. It is best **freshly** killed. The colour is pale red to pink. Pork is finely textured, lean to slightly marbled with fat. The meat of older animals is dark red and coarsely textured.

For roasting use cuts from the leg, fillet, neck, chump, hand and spring.

For braising use cuts from the shoulder, belly, knuckle, liver, kidneys heart.

For frying and grilling use cuts from the leg, fillet, chops, collar, belly, liver, kidneys, heart.

For boiling use collar, belly, spare rib, knuckle, liver, tongue, heart, kidneys, brains.

Cuts of pork

Knuckle. Short fibred cuts from the front and back lower leg.

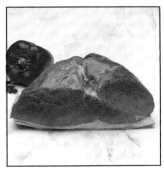

Leg cut. Lean, slightly dry, coarsely textured joint.

Cuts
of Pork

Collar, neck. Juicy cut marbled with fat.

Shoulder, fore slipper.

Loin chops. Fairly lean. Even texture.

American spareribs, spare rib. Continuation of the rib bones from which chops are cut.

Belly, juicy cut with long fibres and streaked with fat.

Fillet. Very tender and lean. Expensive cut.

Ham cut, from the top of the leg, with skin and fat layer.

Leg cut, from the ham. Lean and tender joint.

Leg cut. Very tender cut from the ham. High price range.

Meat

Lamb

Milk lambs are milk fed. Their meat is brick red, finely textured and lean. They are no older then 6 months.

Fattened lambs are not older than 1 year. Their meat is brick red with a little white or pale yellow fat, and is finely textured.

Mutton. This meat is dark red, coarsely textured and has a yellow layer of fat.

For roasting use shoulder, leg and loin or saddle.

For braising use scrag, best end of neck, breast or shoulder.

For frying and grilling use leg, chops.

For boiling use scrag, breast, knuckle, liver, heart, kidneys.

Cuts of Lamb

Best end, scrag. Juicy short fibred cut, streaked with fat.

Shoulder. Slightly sinewy, tender and juicy. Medium price range.

Leg. Relatively lean; very tender juicy cut. Expensive.

Saddle. Juicy cut, often split up into chops.

Shanks. Lower parts of the leg. Lean and streaked with sinews.

Minced meat

Mince can be made from all types of meat. It is extremely sensitive and its storage and sale are subject to very strict rules. Mince can spoil quickly, which is why it should be used shortly after it is bought. The proportion of fat which individual types of mince may contain is specified exactly.

Steak tatare (1). Not more than 6% fat.

Minced beef (2). Not more than 20% fat.

Minced pork (3). Not more than 35% fat.

Mixed mince (4). Not more than 30% fat. This is made from half beef and half pork.

Sausage meat (5) not more than 35% fat. This is prepared from minced pork with added spices, salt and onion.

When shaping mince into meatballs or meat loaf, it needs extra bulk to stop it from becoming too solid.
You can use a soaked and squeezed out bread roll or any of the following:
1 large potato, boiled in its jacket and pushed through the potato press;
1-2 tbs cooked rice or bulgur (cracked wheat);
1-2 tbs quark (also replaces the egg);
2 tbs soaked, drained oats, wheat, barley or rye flakes.

1   2   3   4   5

Mince can be moulded into a variety of shapes, e.g.
meat loaf, hamburgers, rissoles, cevapcici, meatballs, see photo. Wet your hands with water before you shape the mince.

Meat

Offal

In addition to the offal shown in the photo, this group also includes: tripe, lungs melt, udder and stomach. Generally speaking offal is lean and rich in protein, vitamins and minerals. However, it also contains high levels of cholesterol and uric acid. Liver and kidneys are rich in iron and vitamins but since they also contain damaging substances, they should not be eaten too frequently.

Heart
Firm, lean muscle with an outer covering of fat. Lean and rich in vitamins (B-group). Oxheart is largest, weighing around 3 kg. Pig's heart is smaller, weighing only around 500 g.

Veal sweetbreads.
The thymus gland of the calf. This gland only develops during the growth period of young animals. It is white, firm and tender, and must be used quickly as it does not keep well.

Calves' brains
will keep for only a very short time. They are very delicate and have a light consistency.

Liver
The livers of young animals are tender and of a pale colour. Livers from older animals are darker and frequently tough and bitter. Their quality is improved by soaking them in milk which also tenderizes them. Liver is rich in vitamins A, B1, B2 and iron.

Beef liver (1) is dark brown. The cut surface is smooth.

Pork liver (2) is a dark brownish red. The cut surface is finely pored and slightly rough.

Veal liver (3) is a delicacy and is very finely flavoured and tender. Its colour is pale red to brown.

Tip:
Salt liver after it has been cooked. That way it will stay tender.

Kidneys

These are characterized by their elongated, beanlike shape.

Veal and beef kidneys have a visibly corrugated surface and are dark brown (1+2).

Pork and lamb kidneys have a smooth surface and are a reddish grey brown (3+4).

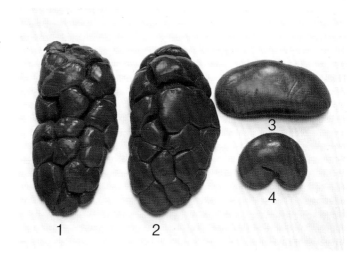

Tongue

All three types of tongue have firm muscle flesh. They can be bought fresh, salted and smoked.

Pork tongue is brownish grey with an almost smooth surface.

Calves' tongue is greyish red with a firm, smooth surface.

Ox tongue is greyish red-violet, it has a rough surface and contains a fairly high proportion of fat. It weighs about 2 kg. It has a pronounced bump.

Meat

Smoked pork loin
(serves 6)

	Wash
1 ½ kg smoked pork loin (bones removed and chopped up)	under cold running water, pat dry and cut a diamond pattern into the fat covering. Peel
1 medium sized onion	Wash
1 medium sized tomato	Trim and wash
1 bunch soup vegetables.	Chop these three ingredients. Place the meat with the fat facing upwards into a casserole which has been rinsed with water, add the vegetables and bones and put the casserole into the preheated oven. As soon as the pan juices start to brown add
a little hot water	Baste the meat occasionally with the pan juices, occasionally replacing evaporated liquid with hot water. 30 minutes before the end of cooking time add
1 small bay leaf 4 cloves	to the casserole. Leave the cooked meat to rest for 10 minutes before carving it. Carve it into slices and serve on a warmed plate. Boil up the pan juices with a little water, strain through a sieve and make up to 500 ml (½ l) with water. Bring to the boil on the top of the stove. Stir in
25 g white flour ½ pot (75 g) crème fraîche (30 % fat) salt pepper	to thicken the liquid. Season to taste with
Electricity:	200-225
Gas:	3-4
Cooking time:	50 – 60 minutes

P: 40 g, F: 58 g, Ch: 7 g, kJ: 3142, kcal: 751.

Accompaniments: Boiled potatoes, sauerkraut with pineapple.

Tip: This dish can also be cooked in a casserole on the top of the oven.

Marinated beef (Sauerbraten)

	Wash
750 g beef (from the hindquarter, without bone)	under cold running water, pat dry and place in a bowl.
	For the marinade peel and slice
2 medium sized onions	Trim, wash and chop
2 bunches of soup vegetables	Add the ingredients to the meat along with
5 juniper berries	
15 peppercorns	
5 allspice berries (Jamaica pepper)	
1 bay leaf	Mix together
250 ml (¼ l) wine vinegar	
375 ml (⅜ l) water	and pour over the meat (the meat must be covered). Cover and leave to stand for about 4 days in a cool place, turning the meat occasionally. When marinating has finished, dry the meat well. Heat
30 g vegetable fat	Brown the meat on all sides in the fat, sprinkle with
salt	
pepper	Add
50 g cleaned raisins	Fry with the meat. Measure
375 ml (⅜ l) marinade	Add
125 ml (⅛ l) water	Pour a little of the mixture into the pan with the meat. Leave the meat to braise, turning it occasionally. Replace evaporated liquid. Wash and chop
2 tomatoes	Crumble
100 g pumpernickel (rye bread)	Add both these ingredients after 1 hour cooking time. When the meat is cooked, leave it for 10 minutes to rest before carving it, to give the meat juices time to settle. Carve the meat into slices and serve on a warmed plate. Strain the pan juices through a sieve and make up to 375 ml (⅜ l) with water. Bring to the boil. Thicken with
dark gravy thickener	Season with salt and pepper
Cooking time:	Approx. 2 ½ hours

P: 43 g, F: 22 g, Ch: 56 g, kJ: 2616, kcal: 623.

Accompaniments: Stewed dried fruit, macaroni or boiled potatoes, red cabbage.

Meat

Smoked pork loin in puff pastry

	Thaw
300 g frozen puff pastry	at room temperature. Thaw
150 g frozen spinach	Wash
800 g smoked pork loin (without bone)	under cold running water, pat dry. Heat
3 tbs cooking oil	Fry the meat in the oil on all sides. Leave to cool off. Peel and dice
2 shallots	
1 clove of garlic	Melt
50 g butter	Sweat the shallot and garlic in the butter, add the well drained spinach and cook gently for about 10 minutes. Season with
salt, pepper grated nutmeg	Leave to cool off. Cover the meat with the mixture (photo 1). Lay 2 pieces of pastry next to each other on a floured pastry board and roll out to make one sheet of pastry. Place the meat and spinach mass on it and carefully wrap the pastry around it (photo 2). Press the edges down firmly. Beat together
1 egg yolk 2 tbs milk	Brush the pastry with this mixture. Cut out some decorations from the leftover pastry and garnish the top (photo 3). Brush the pastry decorations with beaten egg. Place the meat and pastry parcel on a baking sheet that has been rinsed with cold water and put it into the preheated oven.
Electricity:	175-200
Gas:	3-4
Cooking time:	Approx. 45 minutes

continued on page 110

Meat

For the sauce
mix together

1 pot (150 g) crème fraîche (30 % fat)
½ pot (75 g) low fat yoghurt
2-3 tbs mixed chopped herbs Season to taste with
salt
pepper
lemon juice Serve with the sliced meat.

P: 49 g, F: 88 g, Ch: 28 g, kJ: 4826, kcal: 1160.

Boiled brisket

Wash
500 g beef bones under cold running water. Put them into a pan with
1 ½ l cold salted water Boil for about 1 hour. Wash
500 g brisket (without bones) under cold running water. Peel
1 medium sized onion Trim and wash
1 bunch soup vegetables Put the ingredients and meat into the stock with
2 bay leaves Simmer until tender, remove from liquid. Slice the meat and
serve on a warmed plate with a little of the hot stock.
Garnish with the chopped soup vegetables
Cooking time: Approx. 2 ½ hours

P: 28 g, F: 33 g, Ch: 4 g, kJ: 1895, kcal: 453.

The calculation includes the stock.
Accompaniment: Steamed vegetables, horseradish, herb sauce, boiled potatoes.

Fillet of beef

Wash
1 kg well hung fillet of beef under cold running water, pat dry, skin and rub with
salt
pepper Brush with cooking oil and place on the wire rack above a baking tin that has been rinsed with cold water. Push into the
preheated oven and roast, turning occasionally.
Leave the cooked meat to rest for about 10 minutes before carving it, to allow the juices to settle. Serve on a warmed plate.

Electricity: 225-250
Gas: 6-7
Cooking time: Approx. 30 minutes
Accompaniment: Broccoli, duchess potatoes.

P: 32 g, F: 15 g, Ch: 0 g, kJ: 1172, kcal: 280.

Tip: Marinate the fillet overnight in a mixture of oil, brandy and herbs. This will make it even more tender.

Roast pork knuckles

Wash
4 pork knuckles
(500 g each incl. bone)   under cold running water, pat dry and rub with
salt
pepper   Place in a baking tin that has been rinsed with cold water and push into the preheated oven.
As soon as the pan juices start to brown add
a little hot water   Baste the meat occasionally with the pan juices and replace evaporated liquid with hot water.
Peel and quarter
3 medium sized onions   Add these to the baking tin about 30 minutes before the end of the cooking time.
Serve the cooked meat on a warmed plate.
Boil up the pan juices with a little water. If necessary strain through a sieve, continue boiling until reduced and serve with the meat.
Electricity: 200-225
Gas: 3-4
Cooking time: Approx. 3 hours

P: 58 g, F: 72 g, Ch: 1 g, kJ: 3929, kcal: 939.

Accompaniment: Sauerkraut, mashed potatoes

Tip: The gravy is more savoury if it is seasoned with mustard. This also makes it more digestible.

Meat

Calves' brains

	Steep
600 g calves' brains	in water until all the blood has leached out (photo 1). Remove skin and veins from the brains (photo 2). Place in
500 ml (½ l) boiling salted water	to which has been added
1 tbs vinegar	Bring to the boil. Skim off foam. Wash
1 bunch parsley	Add to the pot and cook the brains until tender. Drain well and slice (photo 3). Serve on a warmed plate. Pour
browned butter	over
Cooking time:	5-6 minutes

P: 15 g, F: 18 g, Ch: 1 g, kJ: 992, kcal: 237.

Variations:	Calves' brains can also be used to improve ragout fin" if they are to be fried, they should be allowed to cool off in the cooking liquid, drained and sliced and fried with 3 – 4 beaten eggs and garnished with diced tomato.
Accompaniment:	Tomato salad, toast.

Tip: Calves' brains are not always available, so you should order them in advance from your butcher.

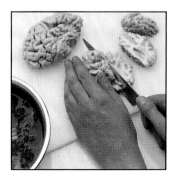

Pork pot roast

Wash

750 g pork (from the hindquarter,
without bone) under cold running water, pat dry. Trim and wash
2 bunches of soup vegetables Peel
6 medium sized onions Finely chop both ingredients. Heat
30 g vegetable fat Fry the meat in it until browned all over.
Sprinkle with

salt
pepper
a little dried marjoram Add a little
hot water Braise the meat, turning it occasionally and replacing
evaporated liquid with hot water.
Add the chopped vegetables 30 minutes before the end of the
cooking time.
Before carving it, leave the cooked meat to rest for 10 minutes
to allow the meat juices to settle.
Carve into slices and serve on a warmed plate.
Push the pan juices and vegetables through a sieve (about 500
ml = ½ l), bring to the boil, reduce if necessary and season with
salt, pepper and marjoram
Cooking time: Approx. 1 ½ hours

P: 34 g, F: 51 g, Ch: 12 g, kJ: 2837, kcal: 678.

Accompaniment: Tomato salad, boiled potatoes garnished with parsley.

Beef pot roast

Wash

750 g beef (from the hindquarter,
without bone) under cold running water, pat dry. Trim and wash
1 bunch of soup vegetables Peel
2 medium sized onions Wash
2 medium sized tomatoes Finely chop the three ingredients. Heat
30 g vegetable fat Fry the meat in it until browned all over. Sprinkle with
salt
pepper Add the chopped ingredients, heat through. Add a little liquid
taken from
125 ml (⅛ l) hot water

375 ml (⅜ l) red wine | Braise the meat, turning it occasionally and replacing evaporated liquid. Before carving it, leave the cooked meat to rest for 10 minutes to allow the meat juices to settle.
Carve into slices and serve on a warmed plate.
Push the pan juices and vegetables through a sieve, bring to the boil and reduce to about 150 ml. Remove from heat. Stir in

100 g soft butter | Reheat the sauce (do not boil), season with salt, pepper,
sugar

Cooking time: Approx. 2 ½ hours

P: 41 g, F: 42 g, Ch: 9 g, kJ: 2745, kcal: 656.

Accompaniment: Savoy cabbage or red cabbage, potato dumplings or boiled potatoes.

Tip: Put the vegetables and pan juices through a food processor. This thickens the sauce and intensifies the taste of the vegetables.

Kidneys in sour sauce

Split open

600 g pork kidneys Cut out the white core, slice, wash, steep in milk for about 2 hours, drain on a colander and pat dry. Heat

50 g butter and fry the kidneys in it until browned all over.
Season with

salt
pepper
sweet paprika powder
dried thyme
dried rosemary Peel and finely dice
2 medium sized onions Add to the pan and brown. Sprinkle on
25 g white flour Allow to brown. Pour over
375 ml (⅜ l) instant stock (cube) and cook the kidneys until tender. Add
2 tbs vinegar Season with
salt
sugar

Cooking time: 10 – 15 minutes

P: 23 g, F: 18 g, Ch: 7 g, kJ: 1247, kcal: 298.

Accompaniment: Rice, macaroni or bread dumplings.

Meat

Veal Cordon Bleu

Lightly beat

8 veal slices (schnitzels)
(about 75 g each) Sprinkle with

salt

pepper Take

4 slices cheese (the size of the
schnitzels, about 40 g each)

4 slices cooked ham (the size of the
schnitzels, about 50 g each) Put a slice of cheese and a slice of ham on to each of 4 schnitzels (photo 1) and cover each with one of the remaining schnitzels. Beat

2 eggs Dip the meat "sandwiches" in the egg and then in

60 g breadcrumbs (photo 2). Heat

60 g margarine and fry the meat in it on both sides (photo 3).

Cooking time: Approx. 10 minutes

P: 56 g, F: 38 g, Ch: 13 g, kJ: 2787, kcal: 666.

Accompaniment: Potatoes baked in foil with cream sauce, peas.

Tip: To prevent the meat from browning too quickly and tasting bitter, shake off any surplus breadcrumbs before frying.

Meat

Floured veal slices

	Turn
4 slices of veal	
(150 g each, cut from the leg)	in
10 g white flour	Sprinkle with
sweet paprika powder	Heat
40 g vegetable fat	Fry the veal in the fat for about 10 minutes until browned all over. Sprinkle with
salt	Remove from the pan to a warmed plate and keep warm. Add
250 g sautéd mushroom slices	to the frying fat and fry for about 5 minutes. Add
5 tbs white wine	
5 tbs double cream (30 % fat)	
1 pot (150 g) crème fraîche (30 % fat)	Season the sauce with
salt	
Worcester sauce	
mustard, pepper	Reduce the sauce and pour over the veal slices.
Cooking time:	Approx. 15 minutes

P: 34 g, F: 30 g, Ch: 6 g, kJ: 1946, kcal: 465.

Accompaniment: Potatoes flavoured with herbs, peas.

Rump steaks with onions

	Peel, cut in half and slice
4 large onions	Make cuts in the fat around the edges of
4 rump steaks (200 g each)	Heat
50 g vegetable fat	Fry the steaks in the fat, turning when one side has browned. Sprinkle with
salt, pepper, steak seasoning	Baste the steaks with the frying fat regularly to keep them juicy. Remove from the pan onto a warmed plate and keep warm. Add the sliced onion to the frying fat, season with salt and pepper, allow to brown, turning frequently
Cooking time for the meat:	6 – 8 minutes
Cooking time for the onions:	8 – 10 minutes

P: 42 g, F: 33 g, Ch: 6 g, kJ: 2188, kcal: 523.

Pepper steaks

	Push the edges of
4 fillet steaks (150 g each)	together to make them thicker. Heat
50 g vegetable fat	Fry the steaks in the fat, turning when one side has browned. Sprinkle with
salt	Crush
2 tsp black peppercorns	Spread over the steaks pressing on firmly. Baste the steaks with the frying fat regularly to keep them juicy.
	Pepper steaks should not be cooked through.
	Remove from the pan onto a warmed plate and pour the frying fat over the steaks
Cooking time	6–8 minutes

P: 29 g, F: 19 g, Ch: 0 g, kJ: 1276, kcal: 305.

Accompaniment: Potatoes baked in foil, cream and herb sauce.

Breadcrumbed pork chops

	Wash
4 pork chops (about 200 g each)	under cold running water, pat dry and beat lightly. Sprinkle with
salt	
freshly ground white pepper	Dip the chops into
2 tbs white flour	
1 beaten egg	
40 g breadcrumbs	in that order. Heat
50 g vegetable fat	Fry the chops in the fat. Serve on a warmed plate
Cooking time per side:	Approx. 8 minutes

P: 23 g, F: 44 g, Ch: 12 g, kJ: 2360, kcal: 564.

Accompaniment: Selection of vegetables, potatoes garnished with parsley.
Variation: Use veal chops instead of pork. The cooking time is then reduced to 5–6 minutes per side.

Tip: To prevent the chops from rising in the middle during frying, cuts should be made in the fatty edge before the chops are coated.

Gratinated pork fillets

	Remove the fat and sinew from
500 g pork fillet (photo 1)	Skin the meat and wash it under cold running water, pat dry and cut into strips. Heat
50 g vegetable fat	and fry the meat in it in portions (photo 2). Sprinkle with
salt	
pepper	Put the meat into a buttered baking dish. Wash and slice
200 g mushrooms	in the frying fat, season with salt and pepper and dust with
10 g white flour	Allow to brown slightly. Add
125 ml (⅛ l) water	
125 ml (⅛ l) white wine	Heat, stirring continuously. Stir in
150 g crème fraîche (30 % fat)	Season with
mustard	
Worcester sauce	Pour over the meat. Grate
20 g Swiss cheese	Sprinkle over the meat (photo 3). Put the baking dish into a preheated oven
Electricity:	200-225
Gas:	4-5
Cooking time:	Approx. 15 minutes

P: 27 g, F: 38 g, Ch: 6 g, kJ: 2155, kcal: 515.

Tip: This dish can be prepared several hours in advance and popped into the oven for gratinating just before serving. However, it will take 5 minutes longer in the oven.

Meat

Meatballs

	Soak
1 stale bread roll	in cold water. Peel and dice
2 medium sized onions	Mix
600 g mixed beef and pork mince	
1 egg	together with the bread roll from which the excess moisture has been squeezed. Season with
salt	
pepper	
sweet paprika powder	With wet hands, form oval meatballs from the mixture. Heat
50 g vegetable fat	Fry the meatballs in the fat until brown all over
Cooking time:	Approx. 10 minutes

P: 27 g, F: 40 g, Ch: 8 g, kJ: 2222, kcal: 531.

Accompaniment: Mashed potato, carrots

Beef olives

	Sprinkle
4 slices of beef	
(150 g each, from the hindquarter)	with
salt	
pepper	Spread with
mustard	Cut
60 g streaky bacon	into strips. Peel and slice
100 g onion	Cut
2 medium sized gherkins	into strips. Place all the ingredients on the beef slices and roll up from one of the narrow ends. Secure with thread or skewers. Heat
40 g vegetable fat	Fry the beef olives in the fat until browned on all sides. Peel and quarter
2 medium sized onions	Trim, wash and chop
1 bunch soup vegetables	Fry these ingredients with the meat for a few moments. Add
a little hot water	Braise the beef olives, turning them occasionally and replace evaporated liquid. Remove the thread or skewers from the cooked beef olives and serve them on a warmed plate. Make up the meat juices to 375 ml (⅜ l) with water. Bring to the boil. Stir together
20 g white flour	

3 tbs cold water	and use to thicken the gravy. Season to taste with salt and pepper.
Cooking time:	Approx. 1 ½ hours

P: 34 g, F: 31 g, Ch: 8 g, kJ: 1971, kcal: 471.

Accompaniment:	Cauliflower, red cabbage, boiled potatoes.
Tip:	Beef olives can be cooked in a pressure cooker. Cooking time is then reduced to 15 minutes.

Veal fricassee

	Wash
600 g veal (without bone)	under cold running water. Cut into cubes and drop into
750 ml (¾ l) boiling salted water	Bring to the boil, skim off foam. Peel
1 large onion	and spike it with
1 bay leaf	
3 cloves	Cook until the meat is tender. Strain off the liquid, measure off 500 ml (½ l)
	for the sauce
	Melt
30 g butter or margarine	Stir in
35 g white flour	Heat until it turns pale yellow. Add
500 ml (½ l) veal stock	Beat well with a whisk and ensure that no lumps form. Bring the sauce to the boil and cook for about 5 minutes. Beat together
1 egg yolk	
2 tbs cold milk	Stir through the sauce, do not allow to boil again. Season to taste with
lemon juice	
salt	
pepper	
sugar	
Cooking time:	45 – 60 minutes
Variations:	Meatballs, cauliflower florets, asparagus pieces, mushrooms, chopped anchovies, can be added as liked.

P: 25 g, F: 17 g, Ch: 7 g, kJ: 1230, kcal: 294.

Accompaniment:	Rice (rice ring mould), asparagus.

Meat

Pork liver

	Wash
500 g pork liver (sliced)	under cold running water and steep in
cold milk	for about 30 minutes (photo 1). Peel and slice
5 medium sized onions	Dry the liver and dip it into
20 g white flour	(photo 2). Heat
40 g vegetable fat	Fry the liver in the fat. When brown underneath, turn and brown the other side (photo 3). Sprinkle with
salt	
pepper	
dried marjoram	Continue cooking until done.
	Reserve the liver on a warmed plate.
	Add the onions to the frying fat, season with salt and pepper and fry until brown, turning frequently. Serve with the liver on the plate
Cooking time for the liver:	6–8 minutes
Cooking time for the onions:	8–10 minutes

P: 26 g, F: 17 g, Ch: 9 g, kJ: 1322, kcal: 316.

Accompaniment: Fried apple rings, mashed potato.
Variations: Use beef or calves' liver instead of pork liver.

Tip: Shake off any excess flour from the liver otherwise an irregular crust will form during frying.

Meat

Meatballs Koenigsberg style

	Steep
1 stale bread roll	in water. Peel and finely dice
1 medium sized onion	Mix together the onion, the squeezed out bread roll and
500 g minced meat (half pork and half beef)	with
1 egg white	
2 level tsp mustard	(photo 1). Season with
salt	
pepper	With wet hands, shape meatballs from the mixture (photo 2). Drop these into
750 ml (¾ l) boiling salted water	Bring to the boil, skim off foam and simmer meatballs until cooked (the water should be just moving). Strain the liquid through a sieve, measure off 500 ml (½ l). For the sauce, melt
30 g butter or margarine	Stir in
35 g white flour	and heat until it turns pale yellow. Add
500 ml (½) l cooking liquid	Beat well with a whisk to ensure that no lumps form. Bring to the boil and cook for 5 minutes. Beat together
1 egg yolk	
2 tbs cold milk	Stir into the sauce (do not allow to boil again). Add
1 tbs capers	
salt	
pepper	
seasoning	
lemon juice	Return the meatballs to the sauce and leave to heat through for 3 – 5 minutes (photo 3).
Cooking time:	Approx. 15 minutes

P: 28 g, F: 39 g, Ch: 15 g, kJ: 2301, kcal: 550.

Meat

Ragout Fin

	Wash
750 g veal	under cold running water. Trim and wash
1 bunch soup vegetables	and put with the meat into
750 ml (¾ l) boiling salted water	Bring to the boil, cook until tender.
	Chop the meat into very small pieces. Strain the liquid through a sieve. Measure off 375 ml (⅜ l).
	For the sauce
	melt
40 g butter or margarine	Stir in
50 g white flour	over heat until pale yellow. Add
375 ml (⅜ l) veal stock	
125 ml (⅛ l) double cream (30 % fat)	Whisk well, ensuring no lumps form. Bring to the boil and cook for 5 minutes.
	Cut up small
100 g sautéd mushrooms	Add to the sauce with the meat, boil up briefly. Add
1 tsp lemon juice	
6 tbs white wine	Season to taste with
salt	
pepper	
Worcester sauce	Divide the mixture among 10 vol au vent cases, sprinkle with
15 g breadcrumbs	
30 g grated cheese	
20 g butter, in pats	Bake in a preheated oven.
Electricity:	225-250
Gas:	6-8
Cooking time:	Approx. 15 minutes

P: 39 g, F: 28 g, Ch: 18 g, kJ: 2222, kcal: 531.

Tip: Ragout fin is a popular filling for vol au vents and rice moulds.

Lamb chops with pineapple

	Remove the fat from
12 lamb chops (60 g each)	Wash the chops under cold running water, pat dry.
	Mix together
3 tbs olive oil	

2 tsp herb flavoured vinegar
½ tsp dried rosemary

1-2 tbs dried basil	Brush the chops with this mixture and leave to stand for about 2 hours. Sprinkle with
salt	Heat
2 tbs olive oil	Fry the meat in the oil on both sides. Remove to a warmed plate and keep warm. Heat
20 g butter	Cut
4 small slices tinned pineapple (130 g each)	in half and fry in the butter. Add
3 tbs sherry	Reduce. Serve the lamb chops with the pineapple slices, pour over the pan juices, garnish with
basil leaves	
Cooking time:	Approx. 10 minutes

P: 22 g, F: 68 g, Ch: 8 g, kJ: 3824, kcal: 914.

Accompaniment: Croquette potatoes.

Goulash

	Wash
500 g lean beef (without bone)	under cold running water, pat dry, cut into cubes. Heat
30 g vegetable fat	Fry the meat in the fat until browned all over. Peel, cut in half and slice
500 g onions	Add to the pan and fry. Season the meat with
salt	
pepper	
sweet paprika powder	Add
2 slightly rounded tbs tomato purée	
500 ml (½ l) hot water	Cook the meat until tender. Add
120 g sautéd mushrooms	Heat through, season the goulash with salt, pepper, sweet paprika powder,
1 – 2 dashes of Tabasco.	
Cooking time:	1 – 1 ½ hours

P: 25 g, F: 11 g, Ch: 12 g, kJ: 1092, kcal: 261.

Accompaniment: Mashed potato, boiled rice, macaroni, tomatoes, cucumber or green salad.

Venison and Game

Rabbit Pot Roast

	Remove the fat from
1 ready to use rabbit (1 ¾ kg)	Cut off the front and back legs and flanks (photo 1). Skin the saddle (photo 2). Wash the pieces under cold running water, pat dry, season with
salt	
pepper	Place
125 g streaky bacon	into a casserole. Trim, wash and chop
1 bunch soup vegetables	and lay on top of the bacon. Add the legs and flanks (photo 3). Brush with butter taken from
30 g melted butter.	Place the casserole into the preheated oven. After about 30 minutes add
125 ml (⅛ l) hot water	Brush the saddle with the remaining butter, add to the casserole and return to the oven. When cooked, leave the meat to rest for 10 minutes to allow the meat juices to settle. Slice the meat on to a warmed plate and keep hot. Heat the pan juices and soup vegetables on top of the stove. Stir in
1 pot (150 g) crème fraîche (30 % fat)	Boil up briefly. Season with salt
Electricity:	Approx. 225
Gas:	3-4
Cooking time:	Approx. 55 minutes

P: 76 g, F: 64 g, Ch: 5 g, kJ: 4079, kcal: 975.

Accompaniments: Boiled potatoes, broccoli.

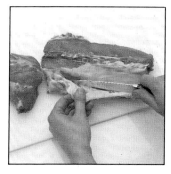

Venison and Game

The meat of venison and game animals is easily digestible, closely textured, lean and rich in protein. There are specific periods during the year in which the various birds and animals may be hunted. The venison that is available in the UK usually comes from roe or red deer. Venison from young animals (up to 3 years of age) is very tender and delicious. Saddle of venison is highly prized – and priced! Wild boar may be available occasionally, and the meat from young animals is delicious. Meat from older animals is fattier, less tender and less easy to digest.

Young hare (up to 8 weeks old) has tender, reddish brown meat. The quality of the meat depends on the age of the animals and their environment.

Preparation

Generally speaking, when game or venison is available in the shops, it has already been skinned and butchered.

Cuts:

1. Saddle, haunch, shoulder. Suitable for roasting and pot roasting.
2. Neck, flank, breast. Suitable for boiling and stewing.

Skinning

The saddle, haunches and shoulders must be skinned before cooking.

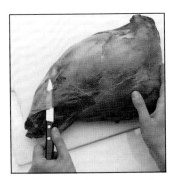

1. Take a very sharp, pointed knife. Slide it carefully under the skin and slit open.

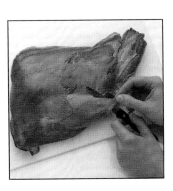

2. Take the cut skin in one hand, holding it just above the flesh.

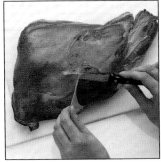

3. Turn the knife blade slightly upwards and remove the skin in a wide strip.

Marinating

Venison is tenderized if marinated before cooking. It absorbs the flavour of the marinade, which gives it a pleasantly spicy taste. The marinade must contain acid (e.g. wine, wine vinegar or buttermilk). Marinating normally takes 12 – 24 hours, but meat can be left for anything from 2 to a maximum of 4 days. If marinating for a longer period, use less seasoning as the meat could otherwise be over seasoned.

Notes:
1. Only meat from **older** animals should be marinated, the meat from young animals is tender and juicy enough.

2. Use enough marinade to cover the meat completely.
3. Do not salt the marinade as this draws out the meat juices and makes the meat dry when cooked.
4. Do not marinate frozen meat. Always thaw it first!
5. Cover the marinated meat and keep it in a cool place until needed.

Cutting hare/rabbit into portions

1. Lay the ready to use hare on its back.
2. With a sharp knife, cut off the front and back legs. Cut

through the joints with steady downward pressure.

3. Cut off the flanks (belly) along the edge of the back with a sharp knife or kitchen scissors.

Bard don't lard!

Barding and larding are done to prevent lean meat from drying out.

Larding. Pulling strips of pork back fat (lardons) through lean meat, game or poultry (using a larding needle). Larding

Barding. Wrapping or covering lean meat, game or poultry with slices of pork back fat, which is tied on or around the meat with twine. The fatty overcoat can be removed after cooking (it is not necessarily meant to be eaten).

damages the meat and meat juices can escape, making the meat dry. For this reason barding is preferable to larding.

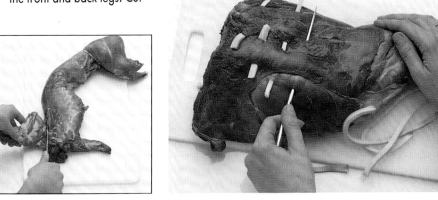

Venison and Game

Carving saddle of hare or venison

1. Place the saddle, bone down, on to a carving board.
2. Cut along the central bone and then along the lower bone to remove the meat.
3. Remove the small fillets on the other side of the bone.

4. Carve into slices.

Note:
If speed is what you need, remove the fillets while raw and then cook. This cuts down cooking time.

Leg of hare

	Remove the skin from
1 ¼ kg legs of hare	Wash under cold running water, pat dry, season with
salt, pepper	
10 crushed juniper berries	Heat
30 g vegetable fat	Fry the hare in the fat until browned all over.
	Peel and chop
3 medium sized onions	Add to the pan with
1 bay leaf	
6 allspice berries (Jamaica pepper)	
a little hot water	Braise the hare, turning it occasionally and replacing evaporated liquid with hot water when necessary. Serve the meat on a warmed plate. Strain the pan juices through a sieve, make up to 375 ml (⅜ l) with water and bring to the boil. Mix
15 g white flour	
125 ml (⅛ l) double cream (30 % fat)	Use this to thicken the liquid, add
3 tbs red wine	Season the sauce with salt and pepper
Cooking time:	1 – 1 ½ hours depending on the age of the animal

P: 56 g, F: 25 g, Ch: 7 g, kJ: 2142, kcal: 512.

Accompaniments: Red cabbage, apple sauce.

Venison steaks in almond flakes

	Lightly beat
4 slices venison	
(150 g each, from the haunch)	Push them together again and sprinkle with
salt, grated nutmeg	Dip the meat in
2 tbs white flour	
1 beaten egg	
80 g almond flakes	(in that order), press the coating on firmly.
	Heat
50 g margarine	Fry the meat until browned on both sides (do not let the almonds get too dark). Arrange on a plate. Boil up the pan juices with a little water and pour over the steaks
Cooking time:	6 – 8 minutes

P: 38 g, F: 24 g, Ch: 7 g, kJ: 1774, kcal: 424.

Accompaniments: Croquette potatoes, pineapple slices with cranberries.

Haunch of venison with raisin gravy
(serves 6)

	Skin (photo 1), wash and dry
1 ½ kg venison from the haunch (without bone)	Mix together
3 tbs cooking oil dried rosemary dried marjoram dried thyme	Brush the meat with this mixture, cover and leave to stand overnight. Sprinkle with
salt	Line a roasting tin which has been rinsed with cold water with half of
100 g sliced pork fat	Place the meat on top of the fat and cover with the remaining slices. Cook in a preheated oven. As soon as the pan juices start to brown add
a little hot water	Baste the meat with the pan juices occasionally and replace evaporated liquid with hot water. Peel
1 medium sized onion	Scrape and wash
1 carrot	Clean
1 leek (150 g)	Roughly chop the vegetables and add to the roasting pan after the first hour of cooking. Slice the meat (photo 2) and arrange on a warmed plate. Boil up the pan juices with water. Make up to 375 ml (⅜ l), bring to the boil (photo 3).

continued on page 138

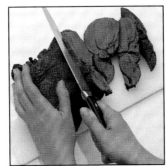
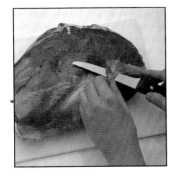

Venison and Game

125 ml (⅛ l) double cream (30 % fat) | Add
50 g cleaned raisins | Mix together
20 g white flour
4 tbs red wine | Use to thicken the gravy
Electricity: 200–225
Gas: 3-4
Cooking time: 2–2 ½ hours

| P: 56 g, F: 32 g, Ch: 12 g, kJ: 2494, kcal: 596. |

Accompaniments: Potato cakes.

Roast haunch of wild boar

Wash

1 ¼ kg wild boar, from the haunch, without bone | under cold running water. Pat dry and rub with

salt, pepper | If the meat has a layer of fat, cut a diamond pattern into it. Put the meat on to the wire rack of a roasting tin, which has been greased with

10 g vegetable fat | with the fatty side facing upwards. Cover with

100 g sliced pork fat | Cook in a preheated oven. When the pan juices start to turn brown add a little liquid taken from

250 ml (¼ l) red wine | Baste the meat occasionally with the pan juices and replace evaporated liquid when necessary. Peel

1 medium sized onion | Trim and wash

1 bunch soup vegetables | Chop both ingredients finely and add to the roasting tin 30 minutes before the end of the cooking time together with

1 bay leaf
10 crushed juniper berries
20 peppercorns
5 allspice berries (Jamaica pepper | Skim off any fat that may have collected. Slice the cooked meat. Arrange on a warmed plate and keep hot. Boil up the pan juices with water, strain through a sieve. Add

2 tbs redcurrant jelly (60 g)
3 lightly rounded tbs sour cream (10 % fat) | If liked, mix together
30 g white flour
cold water
2 lightly rounded tbs sour cream (10% fat)

138

Use to thicken the gravy. Season with salt and pepper

Electricity: 200 – 225

Gas: 3-4

Cooking time: 2 – 2 ½ hours depending on the age of the animal

P: 56 g, F: 11 g, Ch: 14 g, kJ: 1749, kcal: 418.

Accompaniments: Potato dumplings, Brussels sprouts.

Venison ragout

	Wash
800 g venison, from the shoulder, without bone	under cold running water. Pat dry, cut into cubes. Pour
2 tbs port	over it and leave to stand for several hours. Finely dice
75 g streaky bacon	Melt
30 g vegetable fat	Fry the bacon in the fat until crisp. Add the meat and fry until browned all over. Peel, dice and add
1 medium sized onion salt, pepper 4 juniper berries 3 cloves 2 pinches dried thyme 250 ml (¼ l) hot water	Braise the meat until tender, replacing evaporated liquid with hot water as necessary. Wash
250 g chanterelle mushrooms	and add them to the ragout about 10 minutes before the end of the cooking time. Stir in
2 lightly rounded tbs redcurrant jelly (50 g)	Thicken the ragout with
brown gravy thickener	Season with salt
Cooking time:	Approx. 2 hours depending on the age of the animal

P: 44 g, F: 27 g, Ch: 12 g, kJ: 2079, kcal: 497.

Accompaniments: Potato dumplings, boiled potatoes, homemade pasta, red cabbage, apple sauce, cranberry sauce.

Tip: To tenderize the meat and diminish its strong taste, it can be marinated overnight in a mixture of red wine and spices or left in buttermilk for a few days.

Saddle of venison with orange slices
(serves 6)

	Skin (photo 1), wash and dry
1 ½ kg saddle of venison	Rub with
salt, pepper	Place the meat into a roasting pan that has been rinsed with cold water. Wash and dry, cut in half and slice
1 orange (untreated)	Arrange on top of the meat with
75 g streaky bacon (photo 2)	Peel and dice
1 medium sized onion	Scrape and wash
1 medium sized carrot	Wash
1 leek (150 g)	Slice these ingredients and add to the roasting pan, together with the onion and any cutoffs from the meat. Cook in a preheated oven. When the pan juices start to brown add
a little hot water	Carefully baste the meat with the pan juices from time to time and replace evaporated liquid with hot water as necessary. Leave the cooked meat to rest for 10 minutes before carving to allow the meat juices to settle.
	Remove the meat from the bones, discard orange and bacon slices, slice (photo 3), rearrange on the bones and serve on a warmed plate.
	Boil up the pan juices with a little water. Make up to 500 ml (½ l) with water and bring to the boil on top of the cooker. Mix together
30 g white flour	
4 tbs red wine	Use to thicken the gravy. Add
3 tbs orange juice	

continued on page 142

Venison and Game

Garnish the meat with slices of orange
Electricity: 200 – 225
Gas: 3-4
Cooking time: 35 – 50 minutes depending on the age of the animal

P: 41 g, F: 12 g, Ch: 9 g, kJ: 1406, kcal: 336.

Accompaniments: Homemade pasta, croquette potatoes (frozen), bread dumplings, stewed apple with cranberry sauce.

Saddle of hare

	Allow
2 larded saddles of hare (frozen, 1 ¼ kg)	to thaw at room temperature. Cut the meat away from the bones. Break up the bones. Heat
20 g vegetable fat	Fry the bones in the fat. Scrape and wash
1 medium sized carrot	Wash
1 leek	Peel
1 medium sized onion	Roughly chop these vegetables, add to the bones and fry for a few moments. Season with
salt	Add
250 ml (¼ l) water	and boil for 20 minutes. Heat
40 g vegetable fat	Fry the meat in the fat until tender (takes about 15 minutes). Leave to rest before carving to allow the meat juices to settle. Slice the meat and arrange it on a warmed plate. Drain the bones and vegetables on a sieve. Add the liquid to the pan juices. Stir in
1 pot (150 g) crème fraîche (30 % fat)	
4 tbs red wine	Boil until the sauce is reduced and fairly thick. Season with salt
Cooking time:	Approx. 35 minutes

P: 56 g, F: 34 g, Ch: 6 g, kJ: 2485, kcal: 594.

Accompaniments: Mashed potato, homemade pasta, croquette potatoes (frozen), stewed apple with cranberry sauce.

Poultry is divided into three grades: A, B and C. It is available fresh, frozen and thawed and falls into the following groups:

Chicken

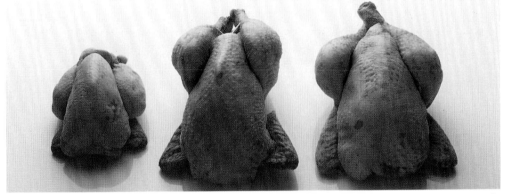

1. **Poussin.** Young fowl, about 5 – 7 weeks old, weighing between 700 and 1200 g. The breastbone is flexible.

2. **Chicken.** Young birds about 8 – 9 weeks old, which are killed before reaching sexual maturity. The breastbone is flexible and they weigh between 1200 and 1500 g.

3. **Capons/boiling fowl.** Birds that are roughly 2 years old. They contain a high proportion of fat. The breastbone is inflexible. Boiling fowl are not specially fattened for killing but are kept for egg laying. Weight: 1500 – 1800 g.

Duck

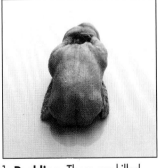

1. **Duckling.** These are killed before they have their adult feathers, at about 7 ½ to 8 weeks. The breastbone is flexible and cartilage has not yet calcified. Weight: 1600 – 1800 g.

2. **Young duck.** Birds about 6 months old which are killed after growing their first adult feathers. The breastbone must still be flexible. Weight 1800 – 2200 g.

3. **Duck.** These are mature birds older than 1 year. The breastbone and cartilage has calcified. Weight: 2000 – 2200 g.

Goose

1. **Young fattened geese.** These birds are killed at about 11 – 12 weeks, before they get their first adult feathers. They have a flexible breastbone and soft cartilage. Weight 4 – 5 kg.

143

Poultry

2. Young goose.
About 6 – 7 month old birds, killed after getting their first adult feathers. The breastbone is flexible and cartilage is soft.

3. Goose.
Birds over 1 year old, killed after reaching sexual maturity. Breastbone and cartilage are calcified.

Note:
Duck and goose are fatty birds.

Turkey

Usually the birds on sale are young birds, no older than 1 year. The breastbone is still flexible and cartilage is not calcified. Turkey meat is lean and rich in protein. **Short fattening** takes 9 – 13 weeks. Weight: 2 – 6 kg (baby turkey). After **long fattening** (22 – 24 weeks) the oven ready birds weigh 5 – 11 kg. These are normally sold in portions.

Plucking poultry

1. Pull the feathers out cleanly. To do this, tighten the skin with the left hand and carefully pull out the feathers without damaging the skin.
2. Remove all quills, if necessary with tweezers.

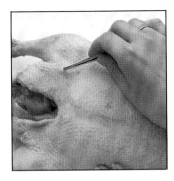

3. Singe off any left over down over a naked flame.

Drawing poultry (gutting)

1. Cut off the head and neck 2 cm above the body.
2. Pull out the crop and gullet.
3. Cut a slit in the belly from the vent towards the breast.
4. Make sure the opening is large enough to allow a hand to be inserted. Carefully remove the intestines and fat. The gall sac must not be injured as the bile it contains will make the meat bitter.
5. Discard the intestines, gall sac and lungs.
6. Wash the bird out thoroughly under cold running water.

7. Drain and pat dry with kitchen paper.
8. Cut open the stomach and remove the thick inner skin.
9. Use the stomach, heart, liver, gullet and wings for soup, stuffings and special recipes.

Cutting up uncooked poultry

Our example shows a chicken.
1. Lay the prepared bird breast-side up. Pull a leg away from body and cut through skin and joint.

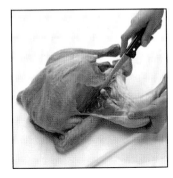

2. Cut through the breast flesh along one side of the breastbone. Split in half with poultry shears.

3. Split through the back along the backbone. Cut out the backbone.
Cut the breast flesh in half.

4. Cut through knee joint to sever the drumstick from the thigh (knife or shears).

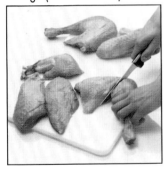

Stuffing poultry

1. Lay prepared bird breast side up.

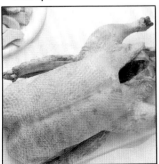

2. Push stuffing into cavity.

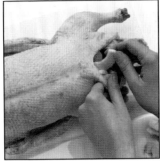

3. Close the opening with kitchen twine or skewers.

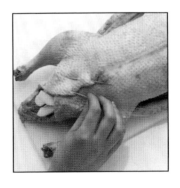

Trussing poultry

Poultry is trussed into the correct shape for roasting so that it cannot dry out during cooking.

1. Lay prepared bird breast side up. Bend the wing tips

back under the body so that they stay there. If the wing tips have been cut off, tie the wings behind the back of the bird with kitchen twine.

2. Tie the legs together with kitchen twine, crossed or uncrossed.

Carving duck or goose

1. Cut through the flesh of the legs down to the joint using a sharp knife. Twist the joint slightly and sever.

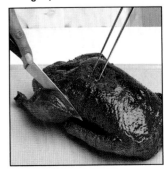

Poultry

2. Sever the wings at the joints.

3. Using a carving knife cut the breast flesh away from the bone on both sides.

4. Slice the breast flesh into portions and arrange on a serving plate.

Thawing poultry

1. Remove all wrapping.
2. Put the bird into a container in which is a drainer insert (preferably not plastic) or an upturned plate.
3. Cover and leave to thaw. The bird may **not** lie in the thawing liquid.
4. Discard all thawing liquid.

5. Wash the thawing container thoroughly in hot soapy water.

Thawing times

	Refrigerator (hours)	Room temperature (hours)
Poussin (about 800 g)	12 – 16	5 – 7
Chicken (up to 1.5 kg)	16 – 23	10 – 15
Duck (2 kg)	25 – 30	14 – 16
Goose/Turkey (4-5 kg)	35 – 38	16 – 20

Barding game birds

Lean birds (e.g. pheasant) are brushed with fat or barded with pork fat slices to prevent the meat from drying out. The bird is then tied up like a parcel (one knot in the length and two across). When cooking is complete the fat is removed and not eaten.

Chipped chicken in cream sauce

	Wash
500 g chicken breast fillets	under cold running water. Pat dry and slice thinly. Heat
30 g vegetable fat	and fry the meat in it in portions. Sprinkle with
salt, pepper	
sweet paprika powder	Drain
150 g sautéd mushrooms	in a colander. Measure off 125 ml (⅛ l) of the liquid. Slice the mushrooms and add to the meat. Add
1 pot (150 g) crème fraîche (30 % fat)	
125 ml (⅛ l) white wine	Stir well and reduce until you have a fairly thick sauce. Season with salt and pepper
Cooking time:	Approx. 10 minutes

P: 30 g, F: 20 g, Ch: 3 g, kJ: 1477, Kcal: 353.

Goose drumsticks in braised cabbage

	Wash
2 goose drumsticks (900 g)	under cold running water, pat dry, sprinkle with
salt	
pepper	Rinse out a braising pan with water. Fry the meat in it until browned on all sides, remove. Remove the outer leaves from
1 kg cabbage	Cut out the stem, wash and drain the cabbage and cut into thin strips. Peel and dice
2 medium sized onions	Add the cabbage and onion to the pan, sauté well, season with salt,
sugar, vinegar	
caraway	Add the drumsticks and
125 ml (⅛ l) water	Braise until cooked. Remove the meat and pop under a hot grill for 1-2 minutes if liked. Season the braised cabbage with salt, sugar and vinegar to taste and arrange on a warmed serving dish with the drumsticks
Cooking time:	Approx. 1 ½ hours

P: 25 g, F: 44 g, Ch: 10 g, kJ: 2389, Kcal: 571.

Chicken fricassee

	Wash
1 oven ready chicken (1 kg)	under cold running water. Put into a pan containing
1 ½ l boiling salted water	Bring to the boil, skim off foam. Trim and wash
1 bunch soup vegetables	Peel
1 medium sized onion	and stick with
1 bay leaf, 1 clove	Add the ingredients to the pan (photo 1). Cook the chicken until tender, remove from the liquid. Strain the liquid, measure off 500 ml (½ l). Remove the meat from the bones, remove the skin, cut the meat into large cubes (photo 2).
	For the sauce
	melt
25 g butter	Stir in
30 g white flour	and heat in the butter until it turns pale yellow. Add
500 ml (½ l) chicken stock	Whisk thoroughly, ensuring that no lumps form, bring to the boil and cook for about 5 minutes. Add
175 g cooked asparagus pieces	
150 g sautéd mushrooms	to the sauce with the meat. Bring briefly to the boil. Add
4 tbs white wine	
1 tbs lemon juice	
1 tsp sugar	Beat together
2 egg yolks	
4 tbs double cream (30 % fat)	and stir into the fricassee (photo 3). Do not allow to boil again. Season to taste with
salt, pepper, Worcester sauce, lemon juice	
Cooking time:	Approx. 1 hour

P: 43 g, F: 24 g, Ch: 14 g, kJ: 2021, Kcal: 483.

Stuffed turkey
(serves 8)

	Wash
1 oven ready turkey (3 kg)	under cold running water, pat dry, season inside and out with
salt	
pepper	(photo 1). Season
250 g sausage meat	with
salt	
pepper	
dried thyme	
dried mugwort	Mix with
1 egg	Rinse
the turkey liver (30 g)	under cold water, pat dry and chop. Peel and finely dice
1 medium sized onion	Heat
20 g margarine	Fry the liver and onion in the fat. Wash, dry, cut in half and deseed
125 g green grapes	Add
1 tbs chopped herbs (chives, parsley)	Mix everything with the sausage meat. Stuff the turkey with the mixture (photo 2). Place the turkey breast side up on the wire rack of a roasting tin that has been rinsed with water. Cover the breast with
125 g streaky bacon slices	Cook on the bottom shelf of a preheated oven As soon as the pan juices start to brown, add
a little hot water.	Baste the turkey occasionally with the pan juices, replacing evaporated liquid with hot water as necessary.

continued on page 152

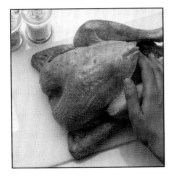

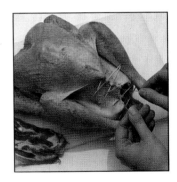

Poultry

	Remove the bacon after about 2 hours. 10 minutes
	before the end of the cooking time, brush the turkey with
cold salted water	Turn the oven up high to crisp the skin.
	Cut the cooked turkey into portions and arrange on a serving
	plate with the stuffing. Keep hot.
	Strain the pan juices through a sieve, make up to 500 ml (½ l)
	with water, bring to the boil on the top of the cooker, boil rapid-
	ly to reduce. Mix together
30 g white flour	
3 tbs cold water	Use this to thicken the gravy. Season with salt and pepper.
	Stir in
2 tbs Madeira	
Cooking time:	Approx. 2 ½ hours
Electricity:	200 – 225
Gas:	3 – 4

P: 65 g, F: 62 g, Ch: 6 g, kJ: 4156, Kcal: 994.

Accompaniments: Bread dumplings, apple sauce with cranberries.

Roast duck

	Wash
1 oven ready duck (about 1 ½ kg)	under cold running water, pat dry, season inside with
salt	Place breast-side up on the wire rack of a roasting tin that has
	been rinsed with water. Cook on the bottom shelf of a
	preheated oven.
	While it is cooking occasionally pierce the skin below the wings
	and leg to let some of the fat escape.
	Skim off the fat which has collected after 30 minutes. As soon as
	the pan juices start to brown, add
a little hot water	Baste the duck occasionally with the pan juices, replacing
	evaporated liquid with hot water as necessary.
	10 minutes before the end of the cooking time, brush the duck
	with
cold salted water	Turn the oven up high to crisp the skin.
	Cut the cooked duck into portions and arrange on a serving
	plate. Keep hot.
	Strain the pan juices through a sieve, make up the gravy with
	water, bring to the boil on the top of the cooker. Mix together
1 – 2 tbs white flour	

2 tbs cold water Use this to thicken the gravy. Season with salt,
pepper
Electricity: 200–225
Gas: 3–4
Cooking time: Approx. 1 ¾ hours

P: 54 g, F: 52 g, Ch: 1 g, kJ: 3050, Kcal: 730.

Accompaniments: Red cabbage, apple slices with cranberry sauce.

Chicken legs in curry sauce

Wash
4 chicken legs (250 g each) under cold running water, pat dry and rub with
salt
pepper Heat
20 g vegetable fat Fry the chicken legs in the fat until browned all over. Remove from the pan. Take

2 medium sized onions
4 medium sized apples
2 slices pineapple (150 g, tin) Drain the pineapple, reserving 200 ml (⅕ l) of the juice.
Dice the ingredients and sauté them in the cooking fat with

1 level tbs curry powder
125 ml (⅛ l) hot water
200 ml (⅕ l) pineapple juice Season with
1 tsp salt Add the chicken legs and braise until tender.
Remove the chicken from the pan, if liked pop under a hot grill for a few minutes. Arrange on a heated serving plate.
Thicken the sauce with
white sauce thickener Season with salt,
curry powder
ground ginger
Cooking time: 25–30 minutes

P: 39 g, F: 12 g, Ch: 40 g, kJ: 1856, Kcal: 443.

Accompaniments: Rice, salads.

Turkey slices with peaches

	Wash
4 turkey slices (125 g each)	under cold running water, pat dry and turn first in
40 g white flour (photo 1)	and then in
1 egg	beaten with
salt	
pepper	
sweet paprika powder	Finally dip both sides in
50 g breadcrumbs	Press on firmly (photo 2). Heat
40 g margarine	Fry the turkey in the fat on both sides (photo 3). Arrange on a warmed plate and keep hot. Plunge
2 peaches (150 g each)	into boiling water (do not allow to boil), refresh under cold water, cut in half, remove the stones and skin. Cut into slices. Melt
20 g butter	Cook the peach slices in the butter. Arrange on the turkey slices
Cooking time:	Approx. 10 minutes

P: 30 g, F: 18 g, Ch: 26 g, kJ: 1724, Kcal: 412.

Accompaniments: Croquette potatoes or rosti.

Tip: Tinned peaches can be used instead of fresh ones.

Poultry

Pheasant in grape sauce

	Cut
1 oven ready pheasant (1 ¼ kg)	into 4 portions. Wash under cold running water, pat dry and rub with
salt	Heat
20 g vegetable fat	in a frying pan and fry the pheasant until browned all over. Cover the pan and cook the pheasant for about 40 minutes. Wash, cut in half, deseed and purée
250 g green grapes	Add to the pan containing the meat about 10 minutes before the end of the cooking time. Remove the meat from the pan to a warmed plate and season the sauce. Stir in
3 tbs red wine	Pour sauce over the meat.
Cooking time:	Approx: 50 minutes

P: 56 g, F: 10 g, Ch: 20 g, kJ: 1736, Kcal: 415.

Roast chicken
(roasting bag)

	Wash
1 oven ready chicken (1 ¼ kg)	under cold running water, pat dry. Mix together
2 tbs cooking oil	
salt, onion-flavoured pepper	
½ tsp sweet paprika powder	Rub the chicken with this mixture inside and out. Place into the roasting bag with
1 bunch soup vegetables	trimmed, washed and chopped. Fasten bag and put into a roasting tin in a preheated oven. When cooked, leave the chicken to rest before carefully opening the roasting bag. Cut the chicken into portions and arrange on a warmed serving plate. Pour the meat juices into a pan, add
125 ml (⅛ l) double cream (30 % fat)	Boil until reduced slightly. Season the sauce with salt and pepper
Electricity:	About 200
Gas:	About 3
Cooking time:	Approx. 50 minutes

P: 49 g, F: 30 g, Ch: 5 g, kJ: 2159, Kcal: 516.

Accompaniments: Chips or fried potatoes.

Roast goose

	Wash
1 oven ready goose (about 3 ¼ kg)	under cold running water, pat dry, rub with
salt, pepper	Place breast-side up on the wire rack of a roasting tin that has been rinsed with water. Cook on the bottom shelf of a preheated oven.
	While it is cooking occasionally pierce the skin below the wings and leg to let some of the fat escape.
	Skim off the fat that has collected after 45 minutes, repeating if necessary. As soon as the pan juices start to brown, add
a little hot water.	Baste the goose occasionally with the pan juices, replacing evaporated liquid with hot water as necessary.
	10 minutes before the end of the cooking time, brush the goose with
cold water	Turn the oven up high to crisp the skin.
	Cut the cooked goose into portions and arrange on a serving plate. Keep hot.
	Boil up the pan juices with water, strain through a sieve, make up to 500 ml (½ l) with water, bring to the boil on the top of the cooker. Mix together
1 level tbs cornflour	
2 tbs cold water	Use this to thicken the gravy. Season with salt and pepper
Electricity:	200 – 225
Gas:	3 – 4
Cooking time:	Approx. 3 hours

P: 40 g, F: 79 g, Ch: 1 g, kJ: 3908, Kcal: 934.

The skimmed fat is included in the calculation

Accompaniments: Potato dumplings, red cabbage.

Variation: Roast the goose with the following stuffing:
Apple stuffing: 1 kg washed apples, unpeeled but cored, or 500 g peeled, sliced apple, 500 g stoned prunes, a little sugar and breadcrumbs.

157

Vegetables

Stuffed onions

	Peel
2 Spanish onions (750 g)	Bring to the boil in
salted water	Boil until half cooked. Cut the onions in half horizontally, hollow out the centre except for about 3 – 4 layers (photo 1), chop the removed onion finely (photo 2).
	Melt
15 g margarine	in an ovenproof dish and sauté the onions in the fat. Stir in
3 tbs double cream (30 % fat)	Season with
salt	Place the hollowed onion halves into the baking dish.
	Mix together
375 g sausage meat	
1 tbs chopped parsley	Stuff the onions with this mixture (photo 3).
	Cook in a preheated oven. Sprinkle the finished dish with
1 tbs chopped parsley	
Cooking time:	Approx. 30 minutes
Electricity:	200 – 225
Gas:	3 – 4

P: 17 g, F: 36 g, Ch: 15 g, kJ: 2021, Kcal: 483.

Serve stuffed onions with mashed potato or potatoes boiled in stock.

Variation: Add 3 – 4 tbs dry white wine to the baking dish together with the double cream.

Vegetables

The increasing consumption of vegetables is in line with recommendations by nutritional scientists that we should eat a higher proportion of carbohydrate and fibre. Vegetables also provide a large proportion of our daily intake of important minerals, vitamins and trace elements. However, it is not only their nutrient content but their flavour and versatility which have contributed to the increased consumption of vegetables. The huge selection of domestic and foreign vegetables in the shops throughout the year allows us to ring the changes with a large variety of vegetable dishes in every season.

Vegetables fall into the following categories:

Root vegetables (e.g. carrots, celery, salsify).
Leaves (e.g. spinach, sea kale).
Shoots (e.g. celery, artichokes)
Brassicas (e.g. cauliflower, cabbage, Brussels sprouts, kohlrabi).
Bulbs (e.g. leeks, onions).
Legumes (e.g. lentils, peas, beans).
Fruit vegetables (e.g. tomatoes).
Squashes (e.g. cucumbers, pumpkins).

Buying and storing vegetables

1. Always buy vegetables as fresh as possible. Wilted leaves and yellow stalks mean that vegetables are not fresh.
2. Vegetables grown out of doors are preferable to vegetables forced under glass. They have more aroma and flavour.
3. If you have to store vegetables, this should be for as short a time as possible, to restrict the loss of nutrients and flavour.
4. Store vegetables in the vegetable drawer of your refrigerator, in a cool cellar or pantry.
5. Root vegetables will keep for up to 5 months if stored in dry sand.

Preparation

Loss of flavour and nutrients can be kept to a minimum if
1. vegetables are washed just before they are prepared;
2. vegetables are always washed **before** being chopped;
3. vegetables are **never** left to stand in water. Vegetables should be washed carefully under cold running water.

Cooking vegetables

1. Choose cooking methods that are as gentle as possible, e.g. **braising** (cooking in

their own juices), **steaming** or cooking wrapped in **foil**.
2. Cook vegetables so that they have some **bite** left. Short cooking times mean that vegetables keep their mineral salts and their fresh colour.
3. Frozen vegetables should **not be thawed** before cooking. Add them to a bed of sautéd, diced onion or drop them into boiling water.

Braising = cooking in very little liquid and water vapour at temperatures under 100°C.

Braising vegetables

1. Put dripping wet vegetables and herbs into a pan.
2. Cover the pan with a close fitting lid.
3. Cook the vegetables on burner setting 1½ – 2 (5 – 6 on automatic burner) on gentle heat. Stop cooking while the vegetables still have some "bite".
4. Add water only if essential. When the liquid is heated, water vapour is given off. This forms condensation on the pan lid, which drips back on to the food. In this circulation the vegetables are cooked at temperatures under 100°C. The flavour, aroma and vitamins are retained. The amount of salt added can be reduced dramatically. The vegetables own water content and the water left over from washing normally provide sufficient cooking liquid.

Vegetable ABC

Aubergine (egg plant).
Long, oval fruit with a smooth, glossy, violet skin. It has little flavour. It need not be peeled. The stalk and any brown marks should be cut away.

Artichoke (globe artichoke).
Firm, green, flower-like heads. They contain cynarin which is effective against liver and gall bladder complaints. Made up of leaves which thicken towards the base and are attached to a fleshy heart. After the heads have been cooked, the leaves are pulled. Only the fleshy base of the leaf is eaten (e.g. dipped in dressing). Before the hearts are eaten, the inedible fibres are removed with a knife.

Cauliflower.
Tightly packed white to cream florets make up the head. The leaves and any brown patches are cut off, as is the stem. The head is divided up and washed. If cauliflower is to be cooked whole, it should be immersed, stem up, in salted water for 2

minutes before cooking to get rid of any insects, etc.

Broccoli.
Greenish violet heads made up of small florets. Not as tightly packed as cauliflower florets. Heads which are yellowed have wilted. Broccoli stems are carefully peeled from the end of the stem up to the florets.

Beans
are available in many varieties (e.g. green, snap and runner). They should never be eaten raw as the beans themselves contain phasin, a protein which can cause inflammation of the stomach and bowel and which is destroyed by cooking. Beans are topped and tailed and any threads removed. They may also be chopped before cooking.

Mushrooms.
Most of the mushrooms available in the shops are cultivated. They have a firm cap, which is attached by its outer skin to the stem. When the weather is moist and warm or mushrooms are no longer quite fresh, the caps open.

Cultivated mushrooms have a white or brown cap. The brown ones have more flavour. The ends of the stems are cut off and the mushrooms are washed under cold running water, chopped or sliced and prepared immediately.

Chicory.
Contains bitter substances that stimulate the appetite. Wilted leaves should be removed and the core, which contains the bitter substances, is removed from larger vegetables and discarded.

Chinese cabbage.
Any wilted leaves are removed, the cabbage split down its length and washed under running water. Tastes only slightly of cabbage.

Peas
are available in several varieties. **Mange tout** (from the French "eat all") are very flat, tender pods that are cooked and eaten pod and all.
Garden peas come in various sizes from very small to large. The smaller the pea the sweeter it is. Garden peas are removed from the pods before cooking.

Vegetables

Fennel.
White fleshy leaves that grow together at the base to form a firm bulb. Has a slight taste of aniseed. Cut off any green stems, brown areas and the feathery tops. The feathery tops can be used. Large bulbs are cut though the middle and washed under cold running water.

Curly kale,
also called collards. This is a member of the cabbage family and has crinkled leaves and a very thick leaf stem. It is best after a frost and contains a high proportion of provitamin A (carotene). Remove thick stems and wilted leaves.

Cucumber.
If grown outdoors, this develops bitter substances near the stem. For this reason cucumbers are peeled from the tip towards the stem. Do not store together with tomatoes as these give off ethylene, a gas which quickly turns cucumber yellow.

Kohlrabi.
Smooth pale green or violet vegetables. Both types are similar in taste. When young, kohlrabi is very tender, but older vegetables can become woody. Kohlrabi contains provitamin A and vitamin C. The pale green leaves may be used in cooking. Stems and wilted leaves should be discarded.

Pumpkins
come in a variety of sizes. Their colour varies from pale yellow to deep orange. They have a firm skin and contain a lot of seeds and fibres. To use the pumpkin, it must be cut open and the seeds and fibrous mass removed.

Leeks
belong to the onion family. They consist of a firm pale to dark green stem with a small root area at the base. Leeks have a sulphur based aroma, are rich in minerals, and are strongly flavoured. The roots are cut off and the leeks are slit in half lengthwise and washed.

Carrots
are strong, pointed roots. They are very rich in provitamin A, a vitamin which, with a little added fat, can be utilized well by the body. Carrots are high in minerals and fibre. The green tops are cut off and the carrots scraped or peeled with a potato peeler.

Horseradish
is a thick root with small roots going off at the sides. It tastes very sharp and contains a large

number of ethereal oils and minerals. Only the length of root to be used is peeled. It should be mixed with a little lemon juice, vinegar or milk after grating to prevent it from going brown.

Sea kale,
also called Swiss chard. Has crisp narrow leaves with a thicker central rib. This vegetable is very rich in vitamins and minerals and has a mild, slightly nutty flavour. Brown marks should be removed and the sea kale thoroughly washed.

Capsicums
occur in many shades of red, green and yellow. They are rich in vitamin C and potassium. The fruits are cut through lengthwise, the white skin and seeds are removed, and the vegetables washed.

Radishes.
Small round to oval roots. Colour varies from red and white to all red. Sharp flavour. The leaves and small roots are removed. There are also larger forms of red, white or black skinned radishes that are not frequently found in the U.K.

Brussels sprouts.
Thick, strong stems bearing miniature cabbages. This is a typical winter vegetable, rich in vitamin C. Any discoloured outer leaves are removed and a cross cut into the base of each sprout to help it cook more evenly.

Beetroot
is a root that is very rich in minerals and vitamins. It contains the pigment glucoside betanin, an important ingredient in food colourings. Beetroot is washed thoroughly and boiled in its skin. It is then plunged into cold water and the skin removed.

Red cabbage.
Crisp tight heads with smooth leaves, slightly crinkled at the edges. Its bluish red pigment, anthocyanin, turns red when acid is added. Remove the wilted outside leaves, wash the cabbage, cut into halves or quarters, remove the stem and chop the leaves very finely.

Asparagus
is a very popular spring vegetable. It has strong white or green shoots with white, green or violet tips. White asparagus grows entirely underground. In green asparagus, the shoots get their colour from exposure to daylight. Cut off the bottom of the shoot, which can be woody, and peel the shoots thinly from the tips downwards.

Spinach
is a leaf vegetable that is rich in minerals and vitamins. Spring spinach has very delicate leaves, autumn spinach is much coarser. The leaves are cut off just above the root and thoroughly washed.

Celery.
Crisp white to green shoots which are sensitive to light and are joined at the base. The ribs are removed individually, washed and any damaged areas removed.

Swedes and turnips.
Firm roots with white to yellow flesh. Rich in minerals and vitamins. Swedes are washed, peeled and chopped before cooking.

Tomatoes.
Firm red fruit vegetables of varying size, shape and flavour. They usually have a juicy core and should be skinned for use in hot dishes.

Green cabbage.
Slightly conical, firm cabbage with leaves that are more tender than those of white cabbage.

Celeriac.
Firm, whitish yellow root vegetable. Rich in vitamins and minerals. Knock on the side with your knuckles, if it sounds hollow it will be soft inside and no good. Celeriac can be washed and peeled before cooking or cooked in its skin, plunged into cold water and then peeled.

White cabbage.
Firm, tight, pale yellowish green heads with looser outside leaves. About half of the harvest is used for sauerkraut. Prepare in the same way as red cabbage.

Savoy cabbage
has a head of looser, lightly crinkled leaves. Prepare in the same way as red cabbage.

Zucchini,
or courgettes, are baby marrows. They are dark green fruits, shaped somewhat like cucumbers and have firm white flesh. Small zucchini are more delicately flavoured than larger ones. Cut off the stem at one end and the flower at the other.

Onions
belong to a very large family. They vary in shape, size, colour and strength. Spring onions are used green shoots and all. Remove the brown or red outer skin of all onions.

Sauerkraut with pork knuckle

	Wash
1 ½ kg pork knuckle	under cold running water, bring to the boil in
250 ml (¼ l) salted water	and boil for about 1 ½ hours. With a fork, loosen
750 g sauerkraut	Peel
1 medium sized onion	and add it to the boiling liquid with
1 bay leaf	
3 cloves	Return to the boil and continue cooking for about 1 hour. Peel, wash and grate
1 large potatoe	Add to the sauerkraut and cook for a few moments to thicken the sauerkraut. Season with
salt	
freshly ground white pepper	
sugar	
Cooking time:	Approx. 2 ½ hours

P: 50 g, F: 85 g, Ch: 12 g, kJ: 4485, Kcal: 1072.

Accompaniments: Mashed potatoes, mashed peas.

Stuffed capsicums (peppers)

	Cut off the stems of
4 large peppers (1 kg)	Slice a lid from the top of each pepper. Remove the white inner skin and the seeds, wash the peppers, dry them and prick the base of each several times with a needle.
	For the filling:
	put
50 g long grain rice (parboiled)	into
250 ml (¼ l) boiling salted water	Return to the boil and cook the rice. It must still be fairly firm. Drain the cooked rice on a sieve, refresh with cold water. Peel and dice
1 small onion	Mix the onion and
1 egg	with
375 g minced meat (half pork, half beef)	Season to taste with
salt	
pepper	

	Fill the peppers with this mixture, put the lids on top.
	Peel and dice
1 small onion	Heat
4 tbs olive oil	Fry the diced onion in the oil. Place the peppers into the pan with the onions. Wash
200 g tomatoes	Cut out the ends, slice the tomatoes and place in the pan. Pour in
375 ml (⅜ l) hot water	Cook the vegetables until tender.
	Remove the peppers and keep warm on a serving dish.
	Push the tomato sauce through a sieve,
	and measure off 375 ml (⅜ l). Bring to the boil and thicken with
white sauce thickener	Add
2 tbs double cream (30 % fat)	Season the sauce to taste with salt,
lemon juice	
Cooking time for the rice:	12 – 15 minutes
Cooking time for the vegetables:	Approx. 50 minutes

P: 23 g, F: 42 g, Ch: 29 g, kJ: 2580, Kcal: 616.

Accompaniments: French bread, green salad.

Ratatouille

	Wash
600 g aubergines	Cut off the stems, quarter, and cut into ½ cm thick slices.
	Cut
1 green and 1 red pepper	in half, remove the stems, seeds and white skin, wash and cut into wide strips. Quarter
4 skinned tomatoes.	Heat
5 tbs olive oil	in an open pressure cooker. Peel and slice
2 onions	Fry the onion lightly in the oil, add the remaining ingredients, season with
salt, pepper	Close the pressure cooker and cook the vegetables. When cooked add
1 peeled, crushed clove of garlic	
1 tbs chopped parsley	
Cooking time:	Approx. 3 minutes

P: 3 g, F: 18 g, Ch: 13 g, kJ: 975, Kcal: 233.

Tip: Ratatouille is a good accompaniment to fried and grilled meat.

Vegetables

Cabbage parcels

	Cut the stem out of
1 ½ kg white cabbage	Place the cabbage in boiling water for a few moments until the outer leaves come loose. Repeat this procedure until all the leaves have come loose. Drain. Cut away the thick ribs until they are flat (photo 1).
	For the filling:
	Steep
1 stale bread roll	in cold water. Squeeze it out well. Peel and dice
1 medium sized onion	Mix with
1 egg	
250 g minced meat (half beef, half pork)	Season with
salt, pepper	Lay 2–3 large cabbage leaves on top of each other, place part of the filling in the centre (photo 2), roll up into a parcel, tying up with kitchen twine or securing with skewers. Heat
75 g margarine	Fry the parcels in the fat on all sides (photo 3), add
a little hot water	Braise the cabbage parcels, turning them occasionally and replacing any evaporated liquid with hot water when necessary. When the cabbage parcels are cooked, remove the twine or skewers and arrange the parcels on a warmed serving plate. Mix together
1 level tsp cornflour	
2 tsp cold water	Use to thicken the cooking liquid. Season with salt
Cooking time:	Approx. 2 hours

P: 19 g, F: 33 g, Ch: 22 g, kJ: 2000, Kcal: 478.

Vegetables

Spinach

	Sort and thoroughly wash (5 – 6 times)
1 kg spinach	Bring to the boil without any added water. Chop finely or coarsely as liked. Peel and finely dice
1 small onion	Heat
25 g butter or margarine	Fry the onion in the fat until pale yellow. Add the spinach
salt, pepper	
grated nutmeg	Cook until tender. Stir in
1 slightly rounded tbs crème fraîche (30 % fat)	Season with salt
Cooking time:	Approx. 10 minutes

P: 6 g, F: 8 g, Ch: 8 g, kJ: 536, Kcal: 128.

Variation: If the spinach is a little bitter, discard the juice and add as much milk as the spinach will absorb.

Cauliflower with white sauce

	Remove the leaves, stem and any damaged parts from
1 medium sized cauliflower (750 g)	Wash under cold running water. Submerge in salted water for a few moments to get rid of any caterpillars or insects. Bring to the boil
250 ml (¼ l) salted water	
250 ml (¼ l) milk (3.5 % fat)	Put the cauliflower stem down into the boiling liquid, bring to the boil, and cook until tender. Transfer the cauliflower to a warmed bowl and keep hot. Measure off 375 ml (⅜ l) of the cooking liquid (make up with milk if necessary). For the white sauce, melt
25 g butter	Stir in
20 g white flour	Stir over heat until the flour turns pale yellow. Whisk in
375 ml (⅜ l) liquid	making sure no lumps form. Bring to the boil and cook for about 5 minutes. Beat together
1 egg yolk	
2 tbs double cream (30 % fat)	Stir this through the sauce, do not allow to boil. Season with
salt, lemon juice	Pour the sauce over the cauliflower and sprinkle with

168

1 tbs chopped parsley
Cooking time for the cauliflower: 25 – 30 minutes
For the sauce: Approx. 5 minutes

P: 17 g, F: 12 g, Ch: 11 g, kJ: 761, Kcal: 182.

Variation: Melt 60 g butter, allow to brown and serve with the cauliflower in place of the sauce.

Tip: The sauce will be more savoury if you add a wedge of cheese spread or 100 g grated Dutch cheese to it.

Fennel with brown butter

Cut off the green stems and remove any damaged parts and brown leaves from
1 kg fennel Cut the root end off straight, wash the fennel and put into
250 ml (¼ l) boiling salted water Cook until tender, cut into quarters and arrange on a warmed serving plate. Melt
75 g butter Allow to brown, season with salt and pour over the fennel
Cooking time: Approx. 40 minutes

P: 6 g, F: 16 g, Ch: 21 g, kJ: 1092, Kcal: 261.

Brussels sprouts

Remove the damaged and brown outer leaves from
750 g Brussels sprouts Cut a piece off the stems and cut a cross into the base of each sprout. Put into
salted water Bring to the boil and cook until tender. Drain in a colander. Melt
50 g butter Shake the sprouts in the butter, season with
salt
grated nutmeg
Cooking time: Approx. 20 minutes

P: 7 g, F: 11 g, Ch: 11 g, kJ: 736, Kcal: 176.

Vegetables

Onions in white wine

	Peel, cut in half and slice
750 g Spanish onions (prepared weight)	Melt
25 g butter or margarine	Lightly fry the onion in the fat until it turns pale yellow. Add
100 ml (⅒ l) white wine	Cook gently until tender. Stir in
2 lightly rounded tbs crème fraîche (30 % fat)	Season the onion with
salt, pepper	Sprinkle with
1 tbs chopped parsley	
Cooking time:	Approx. 30 minutes

P: 3 g, F: 10 g, Ch: 18 g, kJ: 824, Kcal: 197.

Broccoli

	Remove the leaves from
1 kg broccoli	Peel the stems (photo 1), make crosswise cuts in them up to just below the florets (photo 2)). Wash. Bring to the boil
500 ml (½ l) salted water	
grated nutmeg	Add the broccoli, return to the boil and cook until the broccoli is tender. Carefully lift out the cooked broccoli on a slotted spoon and put into a warmed bowl. Keep hot. Melt
75 g butter	Peel and chop
2 hard boiled eggs	Distribute over the broccoli (photo 3).
Cooking time:	15 – 20 minutes

P: 9 g, F: 19 g, Ch: 7 g, kJ: 1044, Kcal: 240.

Vegetables

Green beans
(Snap or runner beans)

	For this dish you can use either the flat, wide variety of runner beans or the round, fleshy pods. Remove the threads from
750 g beans	Wash, slice or snap them. Peel and dice
1 medium sized onion	Melt
25 g butter or margarine	Sauté the onion in the fat until it is golden, add the beans and sauté these for a moment too. Add
125 ml (⅛ l) water	
salt	
pepper	Cook gently until tender. Add
10 g butter	Heat through, season the beans with
salt	
pepper	Sprinkle with
1 tbs chopped parsley	
Cooking time:	Approx. 15 minutes

> P: 5 g, F: 8 g, Ch: 10 g, kJ: 556, Kcal: 133.

Variation:	Add 250 g chopped tomatoes 10 minutes before the end of the cooking time.

Curly kale

	Remove the wilted and brown leaves from
1 ½ kg curly kale	Cut out the thick ribs and wash the kale thoroughly. Bring to the boil in
boiling salted water	Boil for 1 – 2 minutes, drain, chop coarsely. Peel and dice
2 medium sized onions	Heat
30 g lard	Sauté the onion in the lard until it is translucent. Add the kale. Stir in
20 g oats	Heat through. Wash
500 g smoked pork loin	under cold running water, remove the bone and add the meat and bone to the kale. Add
375 ml (⅜ l) water	Season with
salt	Bring to the boil. Cook for about 1 hour. Add
200 g streaky bacon	
2 boiling sausages (150 g each)	to the kale and cook for about 20 minutes. Season the kale with
salt, pepper	

grated nutmeg
sugar   Cut the meat and bacon into slices and serve with the sausages
        and curly kale on a large serving dish
Cooking time: Approx. 80 minutes

> P: 50 g, F: 94 g, Ch: 15 g, kJ: 5201, Kcal: 1243.

Accompaniment: Fried potatoes.

Tip: Curly kale can be cooked in large quantities and frozen in portions for later use. It can also be blanched and then frozen for later use. This dish tastes even better warmed up.

Red Cabbage

Remove the outer leaves from
1 kg red cabbage   Cut the cabbage into quarters, cut out the stem, wash the cabbage and slice or shred very finely. Peel, quarter, core and chop
3 medium sized apples   Melt
60 g lard   Add cabbage and apples and sauté in the fat. Peel
1 medium sized onion   and spike it with
1 bay leaf
a few cloves   Add
salt
sugar
1 – 2 tbs vinegar
125 ml (⅛ l) water   Cook the cabbage until tender. Season to taste with salt, pepper, sugar,
vinegar
Cooking time: Approx. 2 hours

> P: 3 g, F: 16 g, Ch: 21 g, kJ: 1029, Kcal: 246.

Variation: Use white or red wine instead of water. You can also add 1 tbs redcurrant jelly or 2 tbs cranberry preserve. The cabbage can be thickened if liked.

Tip: We recommend cooking red cabbage in large quantities and freezing it in portions for later use. Red cabbage which is to be frozen should have some "bite" left, i.e. it should not be fully cooked.

Braised asparagus

	Wash
1 kg green and white asparagus	Carefully peel the shoots from the tip downwards, being careful not to damage the tips.
	Cut off the ends. Only the lower ends of the shoots of the green asparagus need peeling and the ends must be cut off (photo 1).
	Put
about 750 ml (¾ l) water	into an oval pan, add
salt, sugar	
1 tbs butter	
1 tsp lemon juice	Bring to the boil.
	Place the asparagus on the steaming rack (photo 2) and put the rack in the pan. Steam the asparagus until cooked.
	Arrange the asparagus on a warmed serving plate and keep hot.
	Measure 125 ml (⅛ l) of the cooking liquid for the sauce.
	Mash together
30 g butter	
20 g white flour	Shape into small balls. Squeeze
1 blood orange	Strain the juice through a sieve. Put half the juice with the measured cooking liquid and
100 ml double cream	into a pan and bring to the boil (photo 3). Add the butter and flour balls and simmer, stirring continuously. Add the remaining orange juice to the finished sauce. Add
1 tsp orange liqueur	Season to taste with salt,
white pepper	Serve with the asparagus
Cooking time for the asparagus:	15 – 20 minutes
Cooking time for the sauce:	5 – 7 minutes

P: 5 g, F: 18 g, Ch: 14 g, kJ: 1000, Kcal: 239.

Accompaniments: Rolled fillets of sole, boiled potatoes garnished with parsley

Broad beans with bacon

	Melt
20 g butter or margarine	Cut up
500 g streaky bacon	and fry gently in the fat for about 15 minutes. Wash
750 g podded broad beans (2 ½ – 3 kg with pods)	
1 piece of winter savory	Add to the bacon with
100 ml (⅒ l) water	Cook for about 20 minutes until tender. Remove the bacon and slice it. Season the beans with
salt	Sprinkle with
1 tbs chopped parsley	Serve
Cooking time:	Approx. 35 minutes

> P: 16 g, F: 85 g, Ch: 10 g, kJ: 3874, Kcal: 926.

Leeks

	Trim
750 g leeks (prepared weight)	Cut them into 6 cm lengths and wash thoroughly.
	Melt
25 g butter	Sauté the leeks in the butter. Add
100 ml (⅒ l) water	
salt	
grated nutmeg	Cook until tender. Add
10 g butter	Heat through for a moment, season the leeks to taste with salt and nutmeg, sprinkle with
1 tbs chopped parsley	
Cooking time:	Approx. 15 minutes

> P: 4 g, F: 8 g, Ch: 12 g, kJ: 586, Kcal: 140.

Zucchini, onions and tomatoes

	Peel and cut in half
250 g Spanish onions	Wash, cut in half
250 g zucchini	Slice both ingredients. Wash
250 g tomatoes	

2 tbs cooking oil	Cut out the ends and cut the tomatoes into eighths. Heat Sauté the onions in the oil, add the zucchini slices, cook for about 5 minutes. Add the tomatoes, season with
salt, pepper	
sugar	Continue cooking until done. Season to taste with
salt, pepper, sugar	Sprinkle with
chopped oregano leaves	
chopped basil leaves	
Cooking time:	Approx. 15 minutes

P: 2 g, F: 11 g, Ch: 11 g, kJ: 640, Kcal: 153.

Tip: This vegetable dish is very good with grilled meat and can also be eaten cold with French bread.

Dill cucumber

	Peel
750 cucumber	Cut it in half, and chop it into 2 cm lengths. Plunge
2 medium sized tomatoes	into boiling water (do not allow to boil), then into cold water. Peel, cut out the ends and dice. Peel and dice
2 medium sized onions	Heat
25 g margarine	Sauté the onion in the fat, add cucumber pieces
2 tbs water	
salt	
pepper	Cook gently. Add the tomatoes 10 minutes before the end of the cooking time. Continue cooking until done. Stir in
1 rounded tbs crème fraîche (30 % fat)	Season the vegetables with salt and pepper. Sprinkle with
1 tbs chopped dill	
Cooking time:	Approx. 30 minutes

P: 2 g, F: 8 g, Ch: 5 g, kJ: 410, Kcal: 98.

Tip: Dill cucumber is excellent with grilled meat such as chops and escalopes, and also goes well with meatballs.

Vegetables

Kohlrabi

	Peel, wash and cut into strips
1 kg kohlrabi	Melt
25 g butter	Sauté the kohlrabi in the butter. Add
100 ml (1/10 l) water	
salt	
grated nutmeg	Continue cooking until tender. Add
10 g butter	Heat through, season to taste with salt and nutmeg. Sprinkle with
1 tbs chopped parsley	
Cooking time:	Approx. 15 minutes

P: 3 g, F: 8 g, Ch: 7 g, kJ: 477, Kcal: 114.

Variation: Cook the kohlrabi in 500 ml (½ l) water until tender and then serve in a white sauce.

Young peas

	Wash
750 g podded peas (2 kg with pods)	Melt
25 g butter	Sauté the peas in the butter. Add
100 ml (1/10 l) water	
salt, sugar	Cook until tender. Add
10 g butter	Heat through, season the peas with salt and sugar and sprinkle with
1 tbs chopped parsley	
Cooking time:	Approx. 15 minutes

P: 13 g, F: 8 g, Ch: 24 g, kJ: 971, Kcal: 232.

Gratinated chicory

	Remove any bad leaves from
750 g chicory	Cut a wedge out of the stems to remove the bitter substances. Wash the chicory. Bring to the boil in
salted water	Boil for 5 – 10 minutes (depending on size). Drain well. Wrap each piece of chicory in one slice taken from
300 g boiled ham	Place in a buttered baking dish. Mix together
300 g (2 pots) crème fraîche (30 % fat)	

salt
crushed, dried green peppercorns Stir in
100 g grated cheese Pour the mixture over the chicory. Cook in a preheated oven.
Electricity: Approx. 200
Gas: 3−4
Cooking time: Approx. 35 minutes

P: 26 g, F: 40 g, Ch: 7 g, kJ: 2159, Kcal: 516.

Tomatoes with basil

Plunge
750 g medium sized, firm tomatoes into boiling water (do not allow to boil). Plunge into cold water, remove skins, cut out ends. Melt
40 g butter or margarine in a pan. Stand the tomatoes in the pan and sprinkle with
salt, pepper
chopped basil leaves Cook gently until tender.
Sprinkle the tomatoes with
1 tbs chopped parsley
Cooking time: 10−15 minutes

P: 2 g, F: 9 g, Ch: 6 g, kJ: 477, Kcal: 114.

Carrots

Trim, scrape and wash
1 kg carrots Cut into slices or sticks (leave whole if the carrots are young and tender). Melt
25 g butter Sauté the carrots in the butter for a moment. Add
100 ml (1/10 l) salted water
1 level tsp sugar Cook until tender. Add
10 g butter Heat through briefly.
Season the carrots to taste with salt and sugar. Sprinkle with
1 tbs chopped parsley
Cooking time for young carrots: Approx. 20 minutes
Cooking time for older carrots: 30−40 minutes

P: 2 g, F: 8 g, Ch: 19 g, kJ: 649, Kcal: 155.

Salads

Fennel and orange salad

	For the salad sauce, stir together
2 tbs salad oil	
1 tbs vinegar	
5 tbs water	
3 tbs gin	
sugar	(photo 1). Season with
salt	
pepper	
garlic salt	Wash and trim
500 g fennel	Slice into thin strips (photo 2). Sprinkle with the salad sauce and leave to stand.
	Peel
3 medium sized oranges (150 g each)	and cut them into thin slices. Quarter and arrange in a salad bowl alternating with the fennel. Pour the sauce over (photo 3).

P: 4 g, F: 8g, Ch: 25 g, kJ: 883, Kcal: 211.

Variation: Serve the salad arranged on peeled orange slices.

Salads

Salad plants contain important vitamins, minerals and trace elements. However, it is not only their nutritional value that has made them an essential part of a modern diet; their enjoyment value has also led to an increase in their consumption. The variety of salad plants available has grown immensely.

It is important to use only the freshest, crispest produce for crudités and leaf and vegetable salads. These ingredients are then brought to perfection with a delicious salad dressing.

The most important types of salad plant:

1. **Curly endive**.
   Delicate, feathery, pale green outer and inner leaves. Crisp, fresh, slightly bitter flavour.
2. **Lamb's lettuce**.
   Deep green, small leafed plant. Rich in vitamins (especially provitamin A, vitamin C) and minerals (potassium, iron).

3. **Endive**, escarole. Has a firm, green head with pale yellow heart leaves. The leaves are broad and smooth with a serrated edge.
4. **Cos**
   or Romaine lettuce. Has a firm, green head with longish, narrow leaves and a very slightly bitter flavour.
5. **Radiccio**.
   Fist sized, very firm heads. Dark violet red to light red leaves with white veins. Slightly bitter flavour.

6. **Lettuce**.
   The best known green salad plant. The heads are firm or more loosely packed and delicate. The heart is pale yellow.
7. **Oak leaf salad**.
   Has leaves which resemble those of the oak tree. The leaves harvested in spring are longer than those harvested in summer. They are red, green and slightly violet and have a nutty flavour.

9. **Crisphead lettuce**.
   Firm, crisp, yellowish green heads with tightly packed leaves.

10. **Chicory**.
    Tightly packed bundles of leaves or chicons, white turning to yellow at the tip. The stem at the root end contains bitter substances. Chicory must be protected from exposure to light, which turns it green and bitter.

11. **Chinese cabbage**.
    Long, tightly packed heads with slightly waved leaves and a mild taste of cabbage.

12. **Soy bean sprouts**.
    5 – 6 day old sprouting soy beans (legumes). Tasty, crisp and nutritious sprouts with a neutral flavour.

Note:
In addition to the salad plants listed above, the following fresh vegetables can also be used for salads: carrots, radishes, kohlrabi, horseradish, cucumber, zucchini, cauliflower, capsicums, shredded cabbage.

These are the utensils you will need for preparing salads and crudités:

– Salad basket, bowls, sieves;

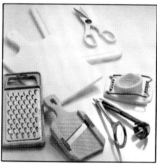

– Vegetable grater, vegetable shredder, egg cutter, chopping board, kitchen scissors;

– Salad bowl, salad servers, lemon squeezer, salt and pepper mills, garlic press, vinegar and oil cruet.

Kitchen herbs

Salad would not be the same without the addition of fresh kitchen herbs. These give the dishes their fresh, finished flavour. Herbs can be used singly or in groups. They can be used to help save salt. In addition, it has long been known that herbs have various beneficial effects on the human metabolism, e.g. they can stimulate appetite (e.g. winter savory, bay leaf), stimulate digestion (e.g. lovage), act as a diuretic (e.g. cress, parsley), help fight colds (e.g. sage), and improve circulation (e.g. rosemary).

Not everyone is in a position to grow their own herbs in the garden, on the balcony or in a window box, but there is usually a good choice of seasonal fresh herbs available at the market or in the shops.

Herbs are also available dried (crushed, ground), frozen, freeze dried or preserved in oil or vinegar.

Salads

Basil, sweet basil.
An annual plant with strong, vertically veined green leaves. The flowers are white to pink. The taste is aromatic, slightly peppery. Fresh: summer to autumn. Excellent with: lamb, poultry, fish, eggs, salads, crudités, vegetables, quark and yoghurt dishes.

Winter savory.
Annual and perennial varieties. Pointed, intensely green leaves. Mauve to white flowers. Fresh: spring to autumn. Use for ragouts, goulash, savoury salads, minced meat, casseroles, grains, pulses and pods, potatoes, vegetables.

Borage.
Annual plant. Longish, slightly hairy, light to dark green leaves and blue flowers. Slight taste of cucumber. Fresh: early summer to autumn. Use for salads, sauces, vegetables, eggs, quark and yoghurt, sandwiches, soups.

Dill.
An annual plant. The stems bear feathery, dark green leaves. Pleasantly spicy. Available most of the year. Use for: crudités, salads, sea food, white poultry and meat dishes, fish, eggs, quark, soups, sauces, pickles.

Tarragon.
Perennial plant. Bushy, many branched shoots. Narrow, long, dark green leaves. Whitish flowers. Fresh: early summer to autumn. Aromatic, slightly bitter flavour. Use for soups, sauces, fish, white poultry and meat dishes, vegetables, grains, eggs, quark, flavouring mustard and vinegar.

Cress.
Tiny green leaves. Strong and spicy taste. Fresh: all year round. Use for soups, sauces, salads, crudités, quark, yoghurt and eggs, herb butter, sandwiches.

Lovage.
Perennial plant. Hollow stem with large, serrated leaves. Very spicy. Use sparingly. Fresh: spring to autumn. Use for soups, casseroles, minced meat, stuffings, stocks, goulash, pods and grains, vegetables, savoury salads.

Mint.
Perennial plant. Many varieties. Pale green and greenish violet, longish, veined leaves. Pale pink to violet flowers. Very spicy flavour. Use sparingly. Fresh: early summer to autumn. Use for minced meat, ragout, stuffings, lamb, goulash, casseroles, legumes.

Marjoram.
Annual plant. Bushy plant with small, oval leaves. White to lilac flowers. Strong flavour, slightly bitter. Fresh: summer to autumn. Use for soups, goulash, minced meat, stuffings, legumes, grains, casseroles, savoury salads, vegetables, potatoes, sausages.

Burnet, salad burnet.
Perennial plant. Slightly feathered leaves of a delicate shade of green. Reddish blue flowers. Mildly spicy, slightly nutty taste. Fresh: spring to autumn. Use for soups, sauces, crudités, sandwiches, eggs, quark, yoghurt.

Rosemary.
Perennial plant, sensitive to frost. Mid to dark green needle shaped leaves. Bluish violet flowers. Strong, spicy, slightly bitter flavour. Fresh: most of the year. Use for roasts, poultry, fish, offal, venison, game, potatoes, grains, legumes, spicy sauces, mushrooms, zucchini, aubergines, tomatoes.

Parsley.
Biennial plant. Smooth and crinkled varieties. The smooth-leaved sorts have a very, strong, spicy flavour. Fresh: all year round. A universal herb. Use for soups, sauces, casseroles, soufflés, pasta, grains, pulses, legumes, quark, yoghurt, eggs.

Salads

Sage.
Perennial plant. Long silver grey to olive green leaves. Bluish violet flowers. Spicy, slightly bitter flavour. Use sparingly. Fresh: spring to autumn. Use for offal, lamb, poultry, eel, grains, pasta, rice, stuffings, tomatoes.

Chives.
Perennial plant. Hollow stalk-like leaves. Bluish violet flower heads. Sharp oniony taste. Fresh: all year round. Universal herb. Use for soups, sauces, herb butter, salads, pasta, rice, vegetables, casseroles, eggs, quark, yoghurt.

Dock.
Normally found in the wild. Long, arrow shaped, strong leaves. Slightly sour flavour. Fresh: spring to autumn. Use for soups, sauces, fish, white meat, poultry, eggs, quark, yoghurt, potato salad, herb butter.

Chinese parsley.
Annual plant. Small, slightly serrated leaves. Very aromatic and spicy. Fresh: summer to late summer. Use for soups, sauces, salads, crudités, casseroles, stocks, legumes, pulses, grains, minced meat, quark, yoghurt, vegetables, potatoes, pasta.

Thyme.
Perennial plant. Very bushy. Small greyish green leaves. Pinkish violet flowers. Fresh: spring to autumn. Use for meat, poultry, venison and game, fish, minced meat, savoury salads, legumes, pulses and grains, vegetables, herb vinegar.

Lemon balm.
Perennial plant. Very bushy. Delicate green, egg shaped, slightly hairy leaves. White to pale yellow flowers. Lemony flavour. Fresh: spring to late summer. Use for salads, sauces, herb butter, eggs, quark, yoghurt, tea, refreshing drinks, fruit salads.

Preparing salads

Delicate leafy salads, e.g. lettuce or oak leaf salad:
1. Separate the leaves.
2. Wash carefully in a bowl of water, taking care not to crush the leaves. Do not leave in the water as soluble substances will leach out.
3. Drain in a salad basket or colander.
4. Tear into large or small pieces as required.
5. Add the salad dressing immediately before serving.

Strong leafy salads, e.g. endive or crisphead lettuce:
1. Cut in half, working upwards from the stem.
2. Wash thoroughly under cold running water.
3. Drain in a colander.
4. Tear into pieces or cut into wide or narrow strips, as preferred.

Finely or coarsely grate the prepared vegetables.

Cut prepared vegetables into smooth or wavy slices (special vegetable knife).

Storage and preparation

1. Carefully wash fresh herbs. Store them with their stems in water or loosely wrapped in foil in the refrigerator.
2. To remove the leaves from small-leaved herbs, take hold of the upper part of the stem in one hand and with the other hand strip the leaves off, working from the top down (e.g. thyme, winter savory, marjoram).
3. Do not chop herbs until just before you need to use them, otherwise they will lose their aroma.

Things to know about salad dressings

There are many recipes for salad dressings. The most well known of these is the

Vinaigrette dressing, which is made from 1 tbs vinegar and 1 – 2 tbs good salad oil. It is seasoned with salt, perhaps a little sugar, fresh kitchen herbs, diced onion and a little mustard.
Vinegar is not just sour, it is also aromatic and spicy. For example we have white wine, red wine, apple, herb or balsamico vinegars. The taste of vinegar must not dominate the dressing, but only contribute to the overall flavour. The **oil** which is used should be as neutral in flavour as possible (e.g. sunflower oil or corn oil). A **lemon and oil** dressing, prepared in the same way as the vinaigrette is growing in popularity. **Cream** dressings are made with fresh or sour cream, e.g. 2 tbs double cream and 1 – 2 tsp lemon juice; sour cream and yoghurt can be seasoned with one or two drops of lemon juice. The other ingredients are the same as those in the vinaigrette. Dressings containing **mayonnaise** are very high in fat. They can be mixed with quark, yoghurt, a hot mashed potato boiled in its skin, or low fat sour cream, which lowers their fat content. Ready mixed salad dressings are available in the shops (in tubes, sachets and bottles) in many different flavours.

Salads

Carrot and apple salad

	Trim, scrape and wash
500 g carrots	Peel, quarter and core
250 g apples	Grate both ingredients coarsely.
	For the salad dressing mix together
2 – 3 tbs lemon juice	
1 tsp salad oil	
salt, sugar	Mix the apple and carrot with the dressing and season to taste with salt and sugar

> P: 1 g, F: 2g, Ch: 16 g, kJ: 351, Kcal: 84.

Variation: Add 1 – 2 tbs chopped hazel nuts to the salad.

Bean salad

	Remove the threads from
500 g green beans	Wash them and cut or snap them into 4 cm lengths. Cook until tender in
125 ml (⅛ l) boiling salted water	Drain.
	For the salad dressing, mix together
3 tbs salad oil	
1 tbs vinegar	
salt	
pepper	Peel and finely dice
1 medium sized onion	Add to the dressing with
1 tbs chopped herbs	
(parsley, dill, winter savory)	Add the warm beans to the salad dressing and mix together. Leave the salad to stand for a while before seasoning with salt and pepper.
Cooking time:	Approx. 30 minutes

> P: 3 g, F: 11g, Ch: 7 g, kJ: 594, Kcal: 142.

Tip: The beans should still be hot when mixed with the dressing so that they can absorb the seasoning.

Green salad

2 medium sized heads of lettuce (300 g)

Remove any wilted leaves from

Pull the other leaves off the stalk, tear up the large leaves and leave the heart leaves whole.
Wash the lettuce thoroughly in lots of water, taking care not to crush it. Drain in a colander or shake in a salad basket or kitchen towel.
For the cream dressing mix together

1 pot (150 g) sour cream (10 % fat)
1 tbs salad oil
1 tbs milk (3.5 % fat)   Season with
salt
pepper
sugar   Peel and finely dice
1 medium sized onion   Add to the dressing with
2 tbs chopped herbs
(parsley, dill, lemon balm,
salad burnet, chives).

Mix well and toss the lettuce in the dressing just before serving.

P: 2 g, F: 8g, Ch: 4 g, kJ: 402, Kcal: 96.

Lamb's lettuce

200 g lamb's lettuce

Remove the roots from
Discard any damaged leaves. Cut larger leaves through once.
Wash the leaves thoroughly and drain well.
For the salad sauce mix together

3 tbs salad oil
1 tbs vinegar   Season with
salt
pepper   Stir in
1 tbs chopped herbs
(parsley, chives)   Toss the leaves in the dressing just before serving.

P: 1 g, F: 11g, Ch: 2 g, kJ: 456, Kcal: 109.

Mixed crudités
(Serves 6)

	Plunge
3 small tomatoes	into boiling water (do not allow to continue boiling). Plunge into cold water, peel, cut out the end, slice. Wash, dry, cut through lengthways and slice
½ cucumber (200 g)	Wash, if necessary cut in half, and cut into 1 cm pieces
125 g celery (prepared weight)	Wash, if necessary cut in half and slice (photo 1)
2 small zucchini (200 g)	
	Take
125 g cooked green beans	
125 g cooked carrot sticks	For the dressing mix together (photo 2)
2 pots (150 g each) crème fraîche (30 % fat)	
1 rounded tbs tomato ketchup	
1 rounded tsp mustard	
1 tbs milk (3.5 % fat)	Season with
salt, pepper	Stir in
4 tbs chopped herbs (chervil, lemon balm, dill, chives, parsley)	Arrange all the salad ingredients on a serving dish and distribute the dressing over them (photo 3)

P: 3 g, F: 16g, Ch: 10 g, kJ: 824, Kcal: 197.

Tip: Any combination of vegetables can be used, e.g. fennel, mushrooms, tomatoes, carrots, Brussels sprouts, leeks.

Salads

Kohlrabi salad

	Peel, wash and coarsely grate
1 kg kohlrabi	
	For the dressing mix together
2 rounded tbs crème fraîche (30 % fat)	
3 tbs lemon juice	
salt	
2 tbs chopped herbs	Mix the kohlrabi with the dressing

> P: 4 g, F: 5g, Ch: 9g, kJ: 410, Kcal: 98.

Crisphead lettuce salad

	Remove the outer leaves from
1 medium sized head of crisphead lettuce	Cut the lettuce in half (photo 1) or quarter it, pick off the leaves, wash and drain on a colander or shake in a salad basket or kitchen towel. Peel (photo 2)
1 medium sized orange (150 g)	and separate it into segments, removing the white skin (photo 3). For the yoghurt dressing mix together
1 pot (150 g) yoghurt (3.5 % fat)	
1 tsp salad oil	
1 tbs vinegar	Season with
salt	Mix the lettuce and orange slices with the sauce. Sprinkle with finely chopped radish if liked.

> P: 3 g, F: 3g, Ch: 6g, kJ: 268, Kcal: 64.

Salads

Zucchini and tomato salad

	Peel, cut through lengthways and thinly slice (photo 1)
3 zucchini (500 g)	Plunge
4 medium sized tomatoes	into boiling water (do not allow to continue boiling). Plunge into cold water, peel, cut out the end, slice thinly. Wash and drain (photo 2)
1 box cress (15 g)	
	For the salad dressing mix together
3 rounded tbs yoghurt (3.5 % fat)	
4 tbs double cream (30 % fat)	
1 tbs vinegar	
1 medium sized peeled, grated onion	(photo 3). Season with
salt	
freshly ground black pepper	
ground ginger	Arrange the salad ingredients on
washed lettuce leaves	Add the dressing and serve at once

> P: 4g, F: 6g, Ch: 12g, kJ: 498, Kcal: 119.

Tip: There is no need to peel small, young zucchini. They can simply be washed and sliced unpeeled.

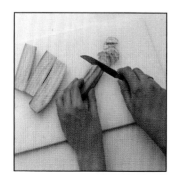  

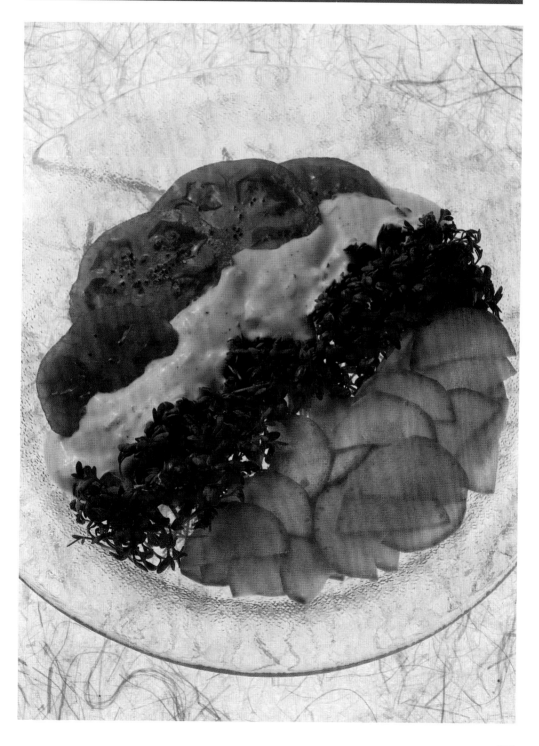

Salads

Red cabbage salad with cranberry sauce

	Remove the coarse outer leaves from
500 g red cabbage (prepared weight)	Cut the cabbage into halves or quarters, cut out the stem, wash the cabbage and shred or cut into very fine strips. Heat
1 tbs salad oil	Sauté the cabbage in it for a few moments, add
a little salted water	Cook the cabbage until half tender. Drain well.
	For the salad dressing mix together
3 tbs salad oil	
2 tbs vinegar	Season with
salt	Peel and finely dice
1 medium sized onion	Add to the sauce with the still warm cabbage. When the salad has cooled off completely stir in
100 g cranberry sauce	Leave to stand for a while
Cooking time:	15 – 20 minutes

P: 2g, F: 14g, Ch: 19g, kJ: 908, Kcal: 217.

Tip: If you prefer the cabbage to be crisp, it can be shredded very finely and used raw or blanched for a moment in hot water.

White cabbage salad

	Remove the coarse outer leaves from
750 g white cabbage	Cut the cabbage into halves or quarters, cut out the stem, wash the cabbage and shred or cut into very fine strips. Mix well with
2 rounded tsp salt	Leave to stand for about 1 hour. Pour off the liquid that has collected after this time.
	For the salad dressing mix together
3 tbs salad oil	
2 tbs vinegar	Season with
salt, freshly ground black pepper	Peel and finely dice
2 small onions	Stir into the dressing. Mix the cabbage with the dressing and leave to stand for a while. Stir in

2 tbs chopped herbs
(parsley, chives, dill).

P: 2g, F: 11g, Ch: 8g, kJ: 590, Kcal: 141.

Tip: This salad can be prepared a day in advance. In this case 1 tsp
caraway seeds is added instead of the chopped herbs.

Cucumber salad

Wash, dry, possibly peel, and finely slice

1 medium sized cucumber (750 g)

For the salad dressing mix together

3 tbs salad oil
2 tbs vinegar Season with
salt
pepper
sugar Peel and finely dice
1 medium sized onion Add to the dressing with
2 tbs chopped herbs (parsley, dill) Mix the cucumber slices with the salad dressing just before
serving.

P: 1g, F: 11g, Ch: 3g, kJ: 485, Kcal: 116.

Variation: Use zucchini instead of cucumber.

Note: Do not salt the cucumber slices as this makes the salad difficult
to digest and also because valuable nutrients are poured off
with the liquid which collects.

Chicory salad

	Remove any bad leaves from
750 g chicory (prepared weight)	Cut the chicory in half, cut out the stems (these are bitter) and cut the chicory into slices about ½ cm wide. Wash and drain well. Cut
150 g boiled ham	into thin strips.
	For the salad dressing mix together
1 pot (150 g) crème fraîche (30 % fat)	
2 rounded tbs tomato ketchup	Season with
salt	
pepper	
sugar	Mix the chicory and ham with the dressing

P: 11g, F: 16g, Ch: 7g, kJ: 954, Kcal: 228.

The salad can be served decorated with whole chicory leaves.

Tip: Chicory salad can be served as a side dish with fish or as a starter with toast and butter.

Potatoes and cereal products

Homemade pasta

For recipe I, sieve ⅔ of
500 g plain flour into a bowl. Make a depression in the centre and put in
1 tsp salt
1 tbs vinegar Slowly stir in
250 ml (¼ l) water working the flour from the sides into the centre. Add the remaining flour. If the dough is still sticky add a little more
plain flour

or for recipe II, sieve
250 g plain flour on to a pastry board. Make a depression in the centre.
Beat together
2 eggs, 1 tsp salt
2 – 3 tbs water Pour into the depression and mix with some of the flour until you have a thick paste. Working towards the centre, quickly combine all the ingredients into a smooth dough.
If the dough is still sticky add a little more
plain flour Break off pieces of the dough (recipe I or II), not too large, and roll them out to the thickness of pasta (photo 1). Lay the rolled out dough sheets on a kitchen towel and leave to dry. When the dough sheets have dried to the stage where they no longer stick together, but not to the stage where they start to break, cut them into the desired width and length (photo 2). Leave the pasta in well ventilated surroundings until completely dry (photo 3)

Recipe I

P: 13 g, F: 1 g, Ch: 93 g, kJ: 1925, Kcal: 460.

Recipe II

P: 10 g, F: 4 g, Ch: 46 g, kJ: 1146, Kcal: 274.

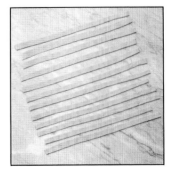

Potatoes and cereal products

The importance of potatoes in our diet is being recognized increasingly. Potatoes contain important vitamins, minerals, nutrients and fibre. Their excellent nutritional properties can best be utilized if they are prepared with a minimum of fat and cooked gently. Different varieties of potatoes have quite different characteristics, which is why it is important to choose the right variety for a particular dish.

Potatoes are divided into 3 categories:
1. **Waxy fleshed varieties** are best for salads, boiled potatoes, potatoes boiled in their skins and fried potatoes.
2. **Slightly floury varieties** are best used for boiled potatoes, potatoes boiled in their skins, fried potatoes, foil baked potatoes, potato dishes.
3. **Floury varieties** are best for potato dumplings, potato pancakes, potato pastry, soups, casseroles, potato cakes.

Storage

In a cool, well ventilated, dark place (4 – 6 degrees C). If potatoes are stored in a warm, light place they will sprout.

Important notes:
- If potatoes are to be boiled in their skins, make sure they are all roughly the same size so that they are all cooked at the same time.
- The same applies to boiled potatoes, which can be cut into pieces of equal size.
- Potatoes boiled in their skins are cooked when the skins come away easily.
- Peel potatoes immediately prior to cooking and put them into cold water so that they do not discolour.
- New potatoes can be eaten with their skins, but should be washed thoroughly.
- New potatoes contain little starch and are therefore not suitable for certain dishes, e.g. potato dumplings, potato pastry.
- Potatoes should be cooked in **very little water**, preferably steamed.

- When the potatoes are cooked, the cooking water should be poured off (use for soups or casserole dishes) and a kitchen towel inserted between the pan and its lid. The residual steam is absorbed by the towel and the potatoes stay dry. Shake the pan occasionally.

Cooking times.
Potatoes boiled in their skins, 20 – 25 minutes depending on size.
Boiled potatoes (quartered), Approx. 20 minutes.
Diced potatoes boiled in stock, Approx. 15 minutes.
Foil-baked potatoes (about 200 g each), 50 – 60 minutes at 200°C, gas mark 3.

Cereal products are products made from grains. They are very important to our diet because they contain important nutrients, vitamins, minerals and fibre. They include rice, rye, wheat, barley, oats, sorghum, buckwheat and maize.

Grains are made up as follows:

Endosperm (mainly starch, containing valuable protein).
Germ (mainly protein but also fat, vitamins and minerals).
Shells (fruit and seed covering).
Husks (e.g. oats and barley).
Grain is sold as:
– wholegrain
– coarsely or finely milled
– crushed (flakes)
– ground (fine, medium fine)

Rice

Rice is rich in vitamins and minerals, low in calories and easily digested. It is the most important staple food of half the earth's population. We differentiate between:
Long grained rice, patna rice. This is frequently used. It has long, slim grains, which look slightly translucent when raw. It remains firm when cooked and is suitable for all savoury rice dishes.
Round grained rice, pudding rice. This exudes large quantities of starch during cooking

and turns very soft and pasty. Suitable only for rice puddings.
Unpolished rice. This has a brownish colour and contains the fine silver membrane with its vitamins and minerals. This rice can turn rancid quite quickly and should be used soon after it is bought. It takes longer to cook than the polished varieties.
It the silver membrane is removed we have **white rice**. The rice grains are cleaned, polished and glazed. This rice contains less vitamins than unpolished rice. The fatty acids have been removed and it can therefore be stored well. In **parboiled rice**, water vapour and pressure are used to push the vitamins and minerals from the silver membrane into the rice grain. These are then retained when the rice is subse-

quently polished. Raw parboiled rice is slightly yellow and turns white when boiled. It retains its firm, separate texture even when reheated.
Fast cooking rice is precooked after polishing. This cuts its subsequent cooking time to 3 – 5 minutes.
Wild rice is the seeds of a species of water grass. It has dark, almost black grains with a nutty flavour. It needs long cooking (at least 40 – 50 minutes) and is very expensive.

Potatoes and cereal products

Preparing rice

1. **Boiling method.** Bring to the boil a large quantity of water with a little oil, salt and an onion stuck with cloves. Cook the rice in the water until it is tender but still has bite. Drain into a sieve, refresh with cold water and drain well. The addition of oil to the cooking water stops it from boiling over.
2. **Absorption method: ratio 1 : 2**
   1 cup of rice to 2 cups of liquid. Fry the rice slightly in a little

oil, season and add the liquid. Cover and leave to swell until all the liquid is absorbed.

Ratio 1 : 1.
1 cup of rice and 1 cup of liquid. This method is suitable for use in a pressure cooker.

Tips for cooking rice

- The cooking time depends on the variety of rice. Unpolished rice needs 35 – 40 minutes, polished rice about 12 – 15 minutes.
- Rice triples in volume during cooking, i.e. 1 cup of uncooked rice will give you 3 cups of cooked rice.
- Cooked rice should not be sticky. The grains will stay separate if a kitchen towel is inserted between the pan and the lid after cooking. The towel absorbs the rising steam and prevents condensation from forming. Overcooking is prevented.
- To serve rice, press it into a soup ladle, buttered rice

mould or cup, and upturn on to a heated plate.
- If you need to heat a large quantity of rice, put it into a buttered baking dish and heat in the oven at 150° C.

- Left over rice can be covered and stored for up to 3 days in a refrigerator. However, it is better to freeze left over rice and to thaw and heat it when needed, in a sieve over water vapour.

Wheat. This is the most important, most frequently used cereal. White flour, which is milled only from the endosperm, and from which the valuable outer layers and the wheatgerm have been removed, has lost a large proportion of its valuable nutrients. Wholewheat flour, which has been milled from the whole grain (without husks), is much more valuable. Wheat is used for all sweet and savoury doughs and pastries, pasta, bread, casseroles, savoury salads, muesli.

Rye. This is the second most important cereal and is mainly used for making bread. It is the darkest of the cereals.

Sorghum. This is a very valuable, small grained cereal. It needs warmth and sandy soil to grow well. It contains many minerals, e.g. magnesium, iron, fluorine, silicic acid. It is good for the skin, hair, nails and teeth. Very versatile. Can be used for sweet and savoury dishes.

Buckwheat. A member of the knotweed family. It has triangular seeds and is an almost forgotten cereal.

Barley. Barley and wheat are the oldest cereals. The endosperm of barley is especially rich in minerals. When barley germinates, large quantities of malt are produced. It is used mainly for beer brewing, but is a cereal that should be used more in cooking.

Oats. Oats have to be husked before use. It is a very valuable cereal and is rich in vitamins, minerals, high quality protein and has a relatively large proportion of high quality amino acids. It is widely used in the diets of babies and children and in dietetics.

Greencorn. This is the half ripe grain of spelt. It is rich in vitamins and minerals and has grown in popularity in recent years. Its typical, savoury flavour is released when it is dried. In Germany it is grown mainly in Franconia and Baden Württemberg.

Spelt. Closely related to wheat. Very high in gluten and popular for making bread.

Maize. This is the most important cereal next to rice and wheat. It contains less protein than the other cereals. In Italy it is made into polenta, in Austria into kukuruz and in Mexico into tortillas.

Wheat

Rye

Barley

Oats

Buckwheat

Greencorn

Spelt

Sorghum

Maize

Preparation/cooking

– The following liquids are suitable for swelling: stock, water with herbs and spices, tomato or carrot juice, milk.

– **Absorption of liquid:** When they swell, the various cereals absorb differing quantities of liquid. The following table shows the recommended amount of liquid per cup of cereal:

Oats	2	cups
Sorghum	3	cups
Wheat	2½	cups
Barley	2½	cups
Pearl barley	3	cups

– **Groats** are available in many varieties. This is coarsely or finely milled cereal. A certain amount of flour is formed during milling. Groats from which the flour has been sieved will give a dish a grainy texture. Groats with flour will give a more homogeneous result.

– All dishes prepared with cereals need plenty of seasoning.

– Many dishes need extra seasoning after cooking.

– When making muesli, cover the soaked cereal and put it in a cool place (e.g. refrigerator), rather than leaving it at room temperature.

Potatoes and cereal products

Pasta

As already mentioned on page 204 (under wheat), from the point of view of nutrition it is advisable to make pasta from wholewheat rather than from white flour. This gives it a far higher nutrient, vitamin, mineral and fibre content and gives it a higher satiation value.
Pasta comes in all shapes and sizes, and Italy is a constant source of innovation. They even have coloured pasta.

Tips for cooking:

- Wrap pasta dough in foil and leave for 30 minutes before rolling it out.
- Cook pasta in plenty of water.
- The addition of a little oil to the cooking water will bind the foaming protein and stop it from boiling over, and it also stops the pasta from sticking together.
- Dried pasta will absorb 2 – 3 times its volume in water during cooking.
- Pasta is best cooked "al dente", which means it should have some bite left.
- Drain cooked pasta on a sieve and serve in a heated serving dish. If you are making a pasta salad, refresh the pasta with water so that it stops cooking at once. Do not leave standing in hot water as this will make it too soft.

- Pasta dough can be coloured, e.g. with tomato purée, puréed spinach, very finely chopped herbs, saffron and beetroot juice.
- Pasta dough can be shaped into spaghetti, broad noodles (fettucini), lasagne or canneloni sheets, ravioli, spirals, shells, etc.
- If you don't want bought spaghetti to break when it is to be cooked, take hold of the spaghetti at one end and slowly dip it into the boiling water. The end that is in the water will soon soften and the remaining spaghetti can be pushed in.
- Dried spaghetti are easily broken. Wrap the uncooked spaghetti in a kitchen towel, take hold of the ends and break the spaghetti into the required lengths against the edge of the table.

Dumplings

In Germany dumplings are made from various basic mixtures, mainly raw or cooked potatoes or bread, but they can also be made from yeast pastry, semolina or greencorn. Depending on the recipe a variety of flavourings can be added to the mixture to make it savoury or sweet. Housewives in Germany can find a whole range of prepared dumplings and dumpling mixtures in the shops. For those who are not so lucky, this book provides the solution.

Tips to make sure your dumplings are a success:

- Mix all the ingredients thoroughly. They must form a homogeneous mass.

- Cook a test dumpling to check whether the consistency of the mixture is right. If it is too **soft** the dumpling will disintegrate. Add more semolina, potato, flour or egg.

- If the mixture is too **solid**, add a little stock, milk, quark or egg.

- **Filling dumplings**: shape a dumpling from the mixture and make a depression in the centre. Put in the filling and carefully close the dumpling around it.

Shaping dumplings

- Small dumplings are made by cutting pieces from the mixture with a moistened spoon.
- Oval dumplings are made with two moistened spoons. Press the mixture between the spoons until it takes on the desired shape.
- Large dumplings are shaped with moistened or floury hands.

- Put shaped dumplings on to a plate that has been moistened with water or a floured board. This stops them from sticking.

Cooking dumplings

1. Bring a large pan full of water to the boil. Dumplings need plenty of room, so the pan should be wide.
2. Slide the dumplings into the boiling water, turn down the temperature and allow to **simmer**. The water should show only slight movement. Do not boil!
3. Dumplings should be cooked in an uncovered pan (except yeast dumplings).
4. Shake the pan occasionally during cooking. The dumplings will turn and rise to the surface.
5. At the end of the cooking time take out the test dumpling and break it open using two forks. If the centre is
   - still moist, allow to cook a little longer
   - dry, the dumplings are cooked.
6. Remove from the water with a slotted spoon and arrange carefully on a warmed serving dish.

Potatoes and cereal products

Fried potatoes

	Wash
1 kg potatoes	Cook in boiling water water until done. Pour off the water, peel the potatoes, leave to cool off, slice.
	Peel and slice
1 large onion	Heat
50 g margarine	in a frying pan. Add the sliced potatoes and onions to the pan, sprinkle with
salt	and fry until browned
Cooking time:	25 – 30 minutes
Frying time:	Approx. 10 minutes

> P: 4 g, F: 10 g, Ch: 38 g, kJ: 1146, Kcal: 274.

Variation: Any left over boiled potatoes can also be fried in this way. First fry 30 g diced streaky bacon in the margarine.

Potato pancakes

	Peel
2 kg potatoes	Peel
1 medium sized onion	Wash both ingredients, grate (photo 1). Mix with
salt, 4 eggs	
60 g white flour (photo 2)	Heat a little oil taken from
250 ml (¼ l) cooking oil	in a frying pan. Put spoonfuls of the mixture into the pan (photo 3), press flat and fry on both sides

> 40 pancakes/per pancake: P: 2 g, F: 7 g, Ch: 9 g, kJ: 435, Kcal: 104.

Accompaniment: Fruit preserve, apple sauce, quark with caraway, bread and butter.

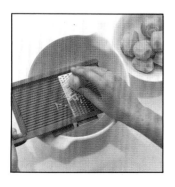

Potatoes and cereal products

Potatoes baked in foil, served with crème fraîche sauce

Wash

4 medium sized potatoes and wrap each one, unpeeled, in a sufficiently large piece of aluminium foil. Bake the foil parcels in a preheated oven

Electricity: 200 – 225

Gas: 4 – 5

Cooking time: 30 – 40 minutes

For the sauce, mix together

1 pot (150 g) crème fraîche (30 % fat)

salt, pepper

1 tbs chopped parsley

a little caraway if liked When the potatoes are cooked, open the foil, break open the potatoes with a fork and fill with the sauce

P: 3 g, F: 11 g, Ch: 16 g, kJ: 782, Kcal: 187.

Tip: Floury potatoes should be used, as these cook through more quickly than the waxy varieties.

Duchess potatoes

Wash, peel, cut in half

750 g potatoes Bring

salted water to the boil and cook the potatoes until tender (about 20 – 30 minutes). Drain, steam dry and mash immediately. Allow to cool off. Mix the mashed potato with

1 egg white

salt, grated nutmeg Put the mixture into a piping bag with a large, star shaped nozzle and pipe puffs on to a greased baking tin. Beat together

1 egg yolk

1 tsp milk Brush the potato puffs with this mixture and bake in a preheated oven.

Electricity: 200 – 225

Gas: 4 – 5

Cooking time: 10 – 12 minutes

P: 6 g, F: 3 g, Ch: 28 g, kJ: 732, Kcal: 175.

Mashed potato

	Wash, peel and cut into pieces
1 kg floury potatoes	Boil in
salted water	until cooked. Drain and mash immediately. Add
75 g butter	
250 ml (¼ l) hot milk (3.5% fat)	Return the pan to the burner and beat the contents until you have a homogeneous mixture. Season with salt and
grated nutmeg	
Cooking time:	Approx. 20 minutes

P: 6 g, F: 18 g, Ch: 40 g, kJ: 1515, Kcal: 362.

Variation: Serve the mashed potato with fried onion rings or browned bread crumbs.

Gratinated potato

	Wash, peel and slice
1 kg potatoes	Slice
250 g sautéd mushrooms	Peel and finely dice
1 medium sized onion	Melt
30 g butter	in a low sided baking dish, sauté the onion and mushrooms in the butter, season with
salt	
pepper	Arrange the potato slices like scales over the mushrooms and onion, sprinkle with salt. Mix together
250 ml (¼ l) double cream (30% fat)	
1 tbs finely chopped chives	Season with salt and pour over the potatoes. Grate
300 g cheese	Sprinkle on top. Cover the baking dish and bake in a preheated oven. Remove the lid about 15 minutes before the end of the baking time
Electricity:	175–200
Gas:	4–5
Cooking time:	Approx. 1 hour

P: 26 g, F: 48 g, Ch: 43 g, kJ: 3100, Kcal: 741.

Tip: Firm fleshed potatoes should be used for gratinated potato.

Potatoes and cereal products

Rice pudding

	Bring to the boil
1 l milk (3.5 % fat)	
salt, 20 g sugar	
lemon peel (untreated)	Add
125 g round grained rice	Stir and return to the boil. Leave over low heat to absorb the milk
Cooking time:	Approx. 40 minutes

P: 11 g, F: 10 g, Ch: 40 g, kJ: 1259, Kcal: 301.

Accompaniment: Melted, browned butter, sugar and cinnamon.

Croquette potatoes

	Wash and peel
750 g potatoes	Boil in
salted water	When cooked, drain and mash immediately (photo 1). Leave to cool. Mix the potato to a dough with
2 egg yolks	
salt, grated nutmeg	Shape rolls from the dough (2 cm thick and 5 cm long). Turn the rolls in
1 beaten egg	
50 g breadcrumbs	in that order (photo 2) and then deep fry in boiling
vegetable fat	until golden (photo 3).
Cooking time for the potatoes:	20 – 25 minutes
Frying time:	2 – 3 minutes

P: 8 g, F: 15 g, Ch: 39 g, kJ: 1419, Kcal: 338.

Variation: Make balls instead of rolls. Make almond croquettes by using flaked almonds (about 100 g) instead of breadcrumbs.

Potato dumplings
(with breadcrumps)

	Wash and boil
750 g potatoes	When cooked, drain, peel and mash immediately. Leave to cool off until next day. Knead in
50 g breadcrumbs	
20 g white flour	
2 eggs	(photo 1). Season the mixture to taste with
salt	
grated nutmeg	With floured hands shape dumplings from the mixture (photo 2). Put the dumplings into
boiling salted water	(photo 3). Return to the boil, turn down heat and simmer until cooked (the water must only move slightly). Drain the cooked dumplings well.
Cooking time for the potatoes:	25 – 30 minutes
Cooking time for the dumplings:	20 – 25 minutes

P: 3 g, F: 1 g, Ch: 14 g, kJ: 343, Kcal: 82.

Serve potato dumplings with marinated beef or roast pork, red cabbage or broccoli.

Potatoes and cereal products

Bread dumplings

	Dice
50 g streaky bacon	Peel and finely dice
2 medium sized onions	Melt
20 g margarine	in a pan and fry the diced bacon in it until crisp, add the onion and fry until translucent. Cut
300 g (about 8) stale bread rolls	into small pieces. Put into a bowl. Heat
300 ml milk (3.5 % fat)	with
30 g butter	Pour over the bread. Mix well. Add the bacon, onion and fat. Beat together
4 eggs	
2 tbs chopped parsley	Season with
salt	With floured hands, form 12 dumplings from the mixture. Put these into
boiling salted water	Simmer until cooked (the water should only move slightly)
Cooking time:	Approx. 20 minutes

Per dumpling: P: 6 g, F: 10 g, Ch: 15 g, kJ: 736, Kcal: 176.

Sweet yeast dumplings

	Sieve
350 g white flour	into a mixing bowl. Mix thoroughly with
1 pkt dried yeast	Add
50 g sugar	
1 pkt vanilla sugar	
salt	
50 g melted, lukewarm butter or margarine	
1 egg	
150 ml lukewarm milk (3.5 % fat)	With an electric mixer with a kneading attachment, knead the ingredients for about 5 minutes, first on the low setting and then on the high setting, until you have a smooth dough. Leave the dough to prove in a warm place until it has roughly doubled in size. Knead again thoroughly. Put
250 ml (¼ l) milk (3.5 % fat)	
10 g butter	into a casserole. Shape the dough into a roll, cut the roll into 8 equal pieces, shape these into 8 dumplings and put them next to each other (not too close) in the milk. Leave in a warm place until

doubled in size. Cover the casserole, bring the milk to the boil.
Turn down the heat and simmer the dumplings until cooked

Cooking time: 20 – 25 minutes

P: 15 g, F: 18 g, Ch: 85 g, kJ: 2452, Kcal: 586.

Tip: Serve with stewed fruit or vanilla sauce. Cold yeast dumplings
can be served for tea with butter and jam.

Béchamel potatoes

	Wash
750 g potatoes	Bring to the boil in salted water. Cook for 20 – 30 minutes
	Drain, peel at once, leave to cool and slice when cold.
	For the béchamel sauce, peel and dice
2 small onions	Dice
40 g smoked ham	Melt
30 g margarine	Fry the ham in the margarine, add
30 g white flour	Stir into the fat with the onion until the flour is pale yellow. Add
375 ml (⅜ l) milk (3.5 % fat)	
125 ml (⅛ l) water	Whisk thoroughly, making sure no lumps form. Bring the sauce to the boil. Cook for about 5 minutes. If preferred the sauce can be passed through a sieve. Add the potatoes, return to the boil and season to taste with
salt	
pepper	
grated nutmeg	Sprinkle with
2 tbs chopped parsley.	
Cooking time:	Approx. 25 minutes

P: 7 g, F: 11 g, Ch: 36 g, kJ: 1184, Kcal: 283.

Tip: A firm variety of potato should be used for béchamel potatoes.
These can be cooked and peeled a day in advance.

Yeast dumplings

	Sieve
300 g white flour	into a mixing bowl. Mix thoroughly with
1 pkt dried yeast	Add
50 g sugar	
1 pkt vanilla sugar	
1 level tsp salt	
50 g melted, lukewarm butter or margarine	
1 egg	
125 ml (⅛ l) lukewarm milk (3.5% fat)	Using an electric mixer with a kneading attachment, knead the ingredients for about 5 minutes, first on the low setting and then on the high setting, until you have a smooth dough (photo 1). Leave the dough to prove in a warm place until it has roughly doubled in size. Knead again thoroughly.

Shape the dough into a roll, cut the roll into 8 equal pieces (photo 2).

With floured hands shape these into 8 dumplings and put them next to each other on a floured board. Leave in a warm place until doubled in size.

Tightly tie a kitchen towel over a wide pan full of boiling water. Tie the cloth to the pan handles. Sprinkle the cloth with flour and lay the dumplings on it (photo 3). Cover with a bowl and leave to cook until done (check with a skewer).

Cooking time: 15–20 minutes

P: 6 g, F: 7 g, Ch: 36 g, kJ: 996, Kcal: 238.

Accompaniments: Melted browned butter, peeled, split, browned almonds, sugar and cinnamon, stewed fruit.

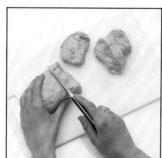

Potatoes and cereal products

Boiled rice

Peel
1 medium sized onion   Bring to the boil in
2 l salted water   Add
250 g long grain rice (parboiled)   Return to the boil and cook the rice at a rolling boil. When cooked, drain the rice in a sieve, refresh with cold water, drain well. Reheat in
30 g butter
Cooking time: Approx. 20 minutes

P: 5 g, F: 7 g, Ch: 50 g, kJ: 1222, Kcal: 292.

Variation: Add a little curry powder to the butter before reheating.

Tip.:   The rice can be cooked a day or several hours in advance. It is then reheated in a little butter in a large covered pan just before serving.

Risotto

Peel and dice
1 medium sized onion   Melt
20 g margarine   Sauté the onion in the margarine, add
250 g Italian round or long grain rice   Cook until translucent. Add
500 ml (½ l) instant stock (cube)   Bring to the boil. Allow the rice to swell until cooked. Do not stir as this will make the rice sticky. Put the cooked rice into a warmed dish and sprinkle with
1 tbs chopped, mixed herbs
Cooking time: Approx. 20 minutes

P: 5 g, F: 5 g, Ch: 50 g, kJ: 1167, Kcal: 279.

Dumplings made with cooked and raw potato
(serves 6)

Wash, bring to the boil and cook
750 g potatoes   Peel, mash immediately and leave to stand until the following day. Grate
500 g peeled, raw potatoes   over a bowl containing water. Strain through a cloth, squeezing out all excess moisture. Add to the mashed potato. Knead in

1 egg
65 g white flour
1 tsp salt   With floured hands form 18 dumplings from the mixture. Put them into
boiling salted water   Return to the boil, turn down heat and simmer very gently until cooked (the water should just move slightly). Drain the cooked dumplings well
Cooking time for the potatoes: 25 – 30 minutes
Cooking time for the dumplings: 15 – 20 minutes

P: 2 g, F: 0 g, Ch: 14 g, kJ: 301, Kcal: 72.

Serve these potato dumplings with beef olives or roast or pot roast pork.

Homemade wholewheat pasta

200 g wheat   Finely grind
Mix together with
2 eggs
2 tbs water
½ tbs vegetable oil
salt, grated nutmeg   using an electric mixer with a kneading attachment, until you have a smooth dough. Leave to stand for a while before rolling out into thin sheets. Place the pasta sheets on a kitchen towel to dry. Cut pasta to the sizes and lengths required and leave spread out in a well ventilated place until completely dry

P: 17 g, F: 9 g, Ch: 23 g, kJ: 1092, Kcal: 261.

Semolina pudding

1 l milk (3.5 % fat)   Bring to the boil
with
salt, 75 g sugar
lemon peel (untreated)
10 g butter   Sprinkle in
125 g semolina   Simmer until cooked, stirring frequently
Cooking time: 10 – 15 minutes

P: 12 g, F: 11 g, Ch: 54 g, kJ: 1561, Kcal: 373.

Casserole dishes

Labskaus (North German speciality)

	Put
600 g lean salted beef	into
500 ml (½ l) boiling water (photo 1).	Cook until tender. Measure off 375 ml (¾ l) of the cooking liquid
	Peel
5 large onions	Coarsely chop the meat and onions before putting them through a meat grinder (photo 2). Melt
75 g margarine	Stir in the meat and onion mixture and heat through for 5 minutes, stirring constantly. Mash
1 kg hot boiled potatoes	(photo 3). Stir into the meat mixture together with
6 tbs liquid taken from a jar of pickled gherkins	
375 ml (⅜ l) beef cooking liquid	Boil up, stirring continuously. Season to taste with
salt	
grated nutmeg	
Cooking time:	Approx. 2 hours

P: 30 g, F: 41 g, Ch: 48 g, kJ: 2950, Kcal: 705.

Accompaniments:	Fried eggs, pickled gherkins or beetroot.
Variation:	Use corned beef instead of beef.

Casserole dishes

Casserole or "one-pan" dishes are among the classics of home cooking. They all have one thing in common, and that is that they are composed of a number of different ingredients, all of which complement one another, cooked together in one pan or casserole. Some are more like richly filled soups, others are a hearty meal in themselves. They are normally eaten as a main course, possibly followed by a dessert. Germany boasts a whole range of regional "one-pan" dishes, such as:
- Pepper pot
- Lentils with sausage
- Potato and apple casserole
- Pichelstein (pork lamb and vegetable casserole)
- Traditional German beef casserole

- Berlin goose casserole
- Beans with pears and bacon

Most other countries also have their special dishes, many of which are already copied in German kitchens:
- Bollito misto (Italy)
- Bortsch (Russia)
- Bouillabaisse (France)
- Paella (Spain)
- Serbian fish casserole (Yugoslavia)
- Paprika duck (Hungary)
- Chop suey (China)
- Boston baked beans (U.S.A.)
- Chili con carne (Mexico)
- Persian lamb pilaw (Iran)
- Irish stew (U.K.)
- Couscous (Tunisia)

Nearly all casserole dishes need long slow cooking. This permits the individual ingredients to transfer their flavours to each other, giving the final, desired flavour. It is always advisable to cook large quantities and freeze portions for future use. Casserole dishes are cooked on top of the stove and in the oven, and always in a pan with a well fitting lid.

You can use your imagination to create new casserole dishes, as long as you remember that all the ingredients need roughly the same amount of cooking time.

Lentils with smoked sparerib

	Wash
250 g lentils	Rinse
500 g smoked pork sparerib	under cold running water. Bring to the boil in a pan with the lentils and
1 ½ l water	Cook until almost soft. Peel, wash and dice
375 g potatoes	Trim, wash and chop
1 bunch soup vegetables	Peel, cut in half and slice
2 medium sized onions	Add the ingredients to the lentils with
125 g smoked sausage	Season with
salt, pepper, vinegar	
dried lovage	Cook until done. Season to taste with salt and pepper. Serve the sparerib and sausage separately or chopped up in the soup. Sprinkle with
2 tbs chopped parsley	
Cooking time:	Approx. 1 ½ hours

P: 37 g, F: 42 g, Ch: 54 g, kJ: 3301, Kcal: 789.

Tip: Lentil soup is ideal for freezing. It is best to freeze it in individual portions and to thaw them fully before reheating. This avoids overcooking the ingredients. When reheating, a little extra liquid can be added if necessary.

Casserole dishes

Smoked pork loin with sauerkraut

	Pour
250 ml (¼ l) water	into a pressure cooker and put the perforated basket into it. Wash
800 g smoked pork loin	under cold running water. Place it in the basket (photo 1). Close the pressure cooker, cook for about 25 minutes, open the pan. Add
750 g sauerkraut	
250 ml (¼ l) water	
25 g pork dripping	
2 cloves	
1 bay leaf	
3 juniper berries	
salt	
sugar	Put the basket on to the lower, perforated basket (photo 2). Close the pressure cooker, cook for about 5 minutes. Cut the cooked meat into slices (photo 3) and serve with the sauerkraut

P: 37 g, F: 35 g, Ch: 10 g, kJ: 2761, Kcal: 660.

Accompaniment: Mashed potato.

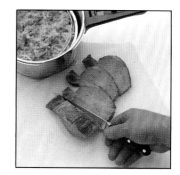

Casserole dishes

Broad bean casserole

	Wash
500 g smoked pork (collar bacon joint)	under cold running water, pat dry and cut into cubes. Peel wash and dice
500 g potatoes	Wash
750 g broad beans	Drain. Heat
40 g margarine	Lightly brown the meat in the fat on all sides. Peel and dice
2 medium sized onions	Just before the meat is sufficiently browned, add the onion, season the meat with
salt, winter savory freshly ground white pepper	Add the diced potato, beans and
500 ml (½ l) water	Cook until tender. Add extra salt if liked.
Cooking time:	Approx. 1 hour

P: 22 g, F: 43 g, Ch: 29 g, kJ: 2602, Kcal: 622.

White bean soup

	Wash
250 g dried white beans	Steep for 12 – 24 hours in
1 ½ l water	Wash
500 g smoked pork (collar bacon joint)	under cold running water. Add to the beans in the steeping liquid, bring to the boil and cook until the beans are almost soft. Remove the cooked meat from the pan. Wash, peel and dice
375 g potatoes	Wash, prepare and chop
1 leek (150 g)	
3 medium sized carrots	
1 piece of celeriac (75 g)	
2 medium sized onions	and add to the beans with
125 g smoked sausage	Season with
salt, pepper	Bring to the boil and cook until all the ingredients are tender. Dice the meat and return to the soup. Sprinkle the soup with
2 tbs chopped parsley	
Cooking time:	Approx. 1 ½ hours

P: 36 g, F: 52 g, Ch: 59 g, kJ: 3740, Kcal: 894.

Pea soup with pork belly

	Wash
375 g unpeeled peas	Steep for 12–24 hours in
1 ½ l water	Wash
500 g smoked sparerib	
250 g pork belly (without bones)	under cold running water. Add to the peas in the steeping liquid and bring to the boil. Cook until the peas are almost soft. Wash, peel and dice
375 g potatoes	Trim, wash and chop
1 bunch soup vegetables	Add these ingredients to the peas, season with
salt, pepper, dried lovage	Bring to the boil. Season the soup to taste with salt and pepper and add the diced meat to it
Cooking time:	Approx. 1 ½ hours

P: 47 g, F: 52 g, Ch: 73 g, kJ: 4222, Kcal: 1009.

White cabbage casserole

	Wash
500 g lamb or mutton	under cold running water. Dry and cut into cubes. Wash and chop
1 kg white cabbage (prepared weight)	Peel, cut in half and slice
2 medium sized onions	Peel and crush
1 clove of garlic (if liked)	Heat
30 g vegetable fat	Lightly brown the meat on all sides in the fat, add the cabbage, onion, garlic and
500 ml (½ l) water	Season with
salt, pepper	
½ tsp caraway	Wash, peel and dice
375 g potatoes	Wash and chop into rings
1 leek (150 g)	Add the vegetables to the pan 30 minutes before the end of the cooking time. When cooked, season the casserole with salt and pepper
Cooking time:	Approx. 1 ¼ hour

P: 28 g, F: 31 g, Ch: 27 g, kJ: 2205, Kcal: 527.

Casserole dishes

Colourful rice casserole with meat

	Wash, dry and dice
500 g pork	Plunge
500 g tomatoes	into boiling water for a moment (do not allow to continue boiling), then plunge them into cold water, peel, cut out ends (photo 1), and cut into quarters.
	Cut
2 large peppers (150 g each, one green, one red)	in half, remove the white inner skin and the seeds, wash the peppers and chop into pieces. Peel and quarter
250 g onions	Dice
60 g streaky bacon	Heat
20 g margarine	Fry the bacon in the margarine until crisp, then fry the meat in the fat until browned on all sides. Add the peppers and onion (photo 2), cook with the meat for about 10 minutes. Season with
salt	
pepper	
2 tbs tomato purée	
a few dashes of tabasco	
sweet paprika powder	
cayenne pepper	Stir in
chopped basil leaves	
chopped lovage leaves	Add
250 ml (¼ l) instant stock (cube)	Cook for 15 minutes then add the quartered tomatoes
250 g parboiled long grain rice	
500 ml (½ l) water	(photo 3). Cook until done. Season to taste
Cooking time:	Approx. 50 minutes

P: 31 g, F: 24 g, Ch: 62 g, kJ: 2607, Kcal: 623.

Casserole dishes

Green bean casserole

	Wash, dry and dice
500 g beef	Remove any threads from
1 kg green beans	Wash them and cut or snap them into small pieces.
	Wash, peel and dice
500 g potatoes	Heat
40 g margarine	Brown the meat on all sides in the margarine.
	Peel and dice
1 medium sized onion	Add it to the pan just before the meat is sufficiently browned, heat through.
	Wash
1 sprig winter savory	Season the meat with
salt	
pepper	Add the savory, beans, potatoes and
500 ml (½ l) water	to the meat and cook until everything is tender.
	Season with salt
Cooking time:	Approx. 80 minutes

P: 30 g, F: 11 g, Ch: 31 g, kJ: 1556, Kcal: 372.

Variation: Dice and fry 150 g bacon, add 2 peeled, diced onions, brown slightly. Add the bacon and onion mixture to the casserole just before serving.

Carrot casserole

	Wash
75 g dried white beans	and steep for 12 – 24 hours in
500 ml (½ l) water	Bring to the boil in the steeping liquid and cook for about 1 hour until tender.
	Wash, dry and dice
500 g pork belly (without bones)	Wash and scrape
750 g carrots	Wash and peel
375 g potatoes	Dice both ingredients. Heat
40 g margarine	Fry the meat in the fat until lightly browned on all sides.
	Peel and dice
2 medium sized onions	Add to the meat just before it is sufficiently browned, heat through.
	Season the meat with

salt
pepper Add the carrots and potatoes and
375 ml (⅜ l) water Cook for about 1 hour until done. Add the beans to the casserole (without the liquid), season with
salt, pepper, vinegar Sprinkle with
2 tbs chopped parsley
Cooking time: Approx. 2 hours

P: 22 g, F: 61 g, Ch: 40 g, kJ: 3519, Kcal: 841.

Variation: Trim one leek, cut it into rings and wash well, and add to the casserole. Cook 1 smoked sausage in the casserole.

Pichelstein casserole

Wash, dry and dice
250 g mutton
250 g pork Scrape and wash
250 g carrots Wash and peel
375 g potatoes Dice these vegetables. Slice and wash
250 g leeks (prepared weight)
250 g white cabbage
(prepared weight) Heat
40 g margarine Fry the meat in the margarine until lightly browned all over. Peel, cut in half and slice
2 medium sized onions Add to the meat before it has fully browned, heat through. Season with

salt
dried marjoram
dried lovage
freshly ground black pepper Add the vegetables, potatoes and
500 ml (½ l) instant stock (cube) Cook until done. Sprinkle with
2 tbs chopped parsley
Cooking time: Approx. 1 hour

P: 27 g, F: 33 g, Ch: 25 g, kJ: 2222, Kcal: 531.

Soufflés and baked dishes

Omelette soufflé

Beat together

4 egg yolks
100 g sugar   until creamy (photo 1). Beat
4 egg-whites   until stiff, add to the egg yolks. Sieve
20 g cornflour   over the mixture and carefully fold in (do not stir) (photo 2).
Pour the mixture into a buttered, low sided baking dish
(photo 3) and bake in a preheated oven

Electricity: Approx. 175
Gas: 2–3
Cooking time: 25–30 minutes
Sprinkle with
20 g icing sugar   and serve at once

P: 7 g, F: 6 g, Ch: 35 g, kJ: 944, Kcal: 223.

Accompaniments: Sugared berries or stewed fruit.

Tip: Omelette soufflé will have a really light consistency if the egg yolks are beaten until really creamy and the egg-whites are really stiff.

Soufflés and baked dishes

There are lots of different recipes for sweet and savoury soufflés and dishes baked in the oven. Generally speaking the ingredients for these dishes are chopped finely and mixed with a semi-liquid mass (sauce) in a baking dish and baked in the oven. This is an ideal way of using up leftovers, e.g. potatoes, pasta, rice, meat, fish or sausage.

A few ideas for savoury baked dishes:

- Mashed potato, smoked fish, sauerkraut, a little cheese.
- Sliced potato, minced meat, cabbage, beaten egg with milk.
- Pearl barley, leeks, cheese, beaten egg with yoghurt.
- Rice, fish, mushrooms, beaten egg-white.
- Pasta, minced meat sauce, cheese.
- Pasta, quark, ham or salami, egg yolks, beaten egg-white.
- Various vegetables, cheese sauce.

A few ideas for sweet baked dishes:

- Semolina, quark, apples or cherries, egg yolks, beaten egg-white.
- Sorghum, milk, cherries, eggs.
- Soaked rusks or cake, any fruit, egg beaten with milk.
- Quark, nuts, egg yolk, ap-

ples, beaten egg-white.
- White bread, eggs beaten with milk, raisins, plums.
- Barley gruel, dried fruit, cream.
- Raisin buns, cherries, egg yolks, milk, beaten egg-white.

Preparation:

1. Carefully butter an oven-proof dish, e.g. earthenware, china or glass.

2. Layer the prepared, chopped ingredients into the dish. For dishes that are supposed to rise during baking, remember to fill the dish no more than ¾ full.

3. Set the oven to the required temperature and preheat, if specified in the recipe.

4. Sprinkle the surface of the food with breadcrumbs, grated cheese, chopped nuts or almonds, or butter pats.

5. Wipe the edge of the dish before it goes into the oven,

since any food adhering to it quickly burns. This causes

food that has risen to collapse.

6. After baking, the container is placed on a heatproof stand and the food is served directly from it.

Lightening things up

Baked dishes of this type should have a light consistency. This can be achieved by the following methods of preparation:
- Pour a sauce over the ingredients, e.g. cheese, minced meat or tomato.

- Pour beaten egg and milk

over the ingredients (beat together 250 ml milk and 1 egg or 500 ml milk and 2 eggs and season).
- Pour a yoghurt and egg mixture over (beat together and season 1 pot of yoghurt and 1 egg).
- Stir egg yolk into the ingredients. Beat egg-white stiffly and fold in carefully.
- Ingredients that are too liquid can be layered with grated or diced cheese.

236

Baked quark pudding

	Mix together
2 pkts vanilla pudding powder	with ⅔ of
200 g sugar	Add
2 ½ egg yolks	with ¼ of
500 ml (½ l) cold milk (3.5 % fat)	Bring the remaining milk to the boil, remove from the heat and stir in the pudding powder. Return to the heat and boil up for a moment. Remove the pan from the heat. Add
750 g quark (low fat)	Stir in and bring to the boil for a moment. Pour the hot milk into a bowl. Stir in
50 g raisins	Beat
3 egg-whites	stiffly, adding the remaining sugar by the spoonful. Fold into the quark mixture, pour into a buttered baking dish, smooth the surface. Beat together
½ egg yolk	
1 tbs milk (3.5 % fat)	Brush the surface with this mixture. Bake in a preheated oven.
Electricity:	175 – 200
Gas:	2 – 3
Cooking time:	60 – 70 minutes

P: 35 g, F: 10 g, Ch: 88 g, kJ: 2843, Kcal: 591.

Sour cherry and quark bake

	Beat together
3 egg yolks	
125 g sugar	until creamy, mix with
75 g semolina	
2 tbs lemon juice	
500 g low fat quark	Stiffly beat
3 egg-whites	and fold carefully into the egg and quark mixture. Drain
460 g stoned, cooked, sour cherries	Stir into the mixture. Transfer to a buttered baking dish and bake in a preheated oven
Electricity:	200 – 225
Gas:	3 – 4
Cooking time:	Approx. 35 minutes

P: 25 g, F: 5 g, Ch: 73 g, kJ: 1870, Kcal: 447.

Soufflés and baked dishes

Snow topped stewed fruit bake

	Heat
250 ml (¼ l) milk (3.5 % fat)	Soak
100 g rusks	in the milk. Drain
200 g stewed plums	
150 g stewed pears	
150 g stewed apples	(photo 1), then pour into a buttered baking dish. Layer the soaked rusks over the fruit, keeping them close together (photo 2).
	Prepare a vanilla pudding from
500 ml (½ l) milk (3.5 % fat)	
1 pkt instant vanilla pudding powder	
50 g sugar	
1 egg	Pour the pudding over the rusks. Beat
1 egg-white stiffly	Sweeten with
1 level tsp sugar	and spread evenly over the pudding (photo 3).
	Bake in a preheated oven
Electricity:	175 – 200
Gas:	2 – 3
Cooking time:	15 – 20 minutes

P: 11 g, F: 9 g, Ch: 74 g, kJ: 1818, Kcal: 431.

Tip: Any left over stewed fruit, canned fruit or preserved fruit can be used for the fruit filling.

Soufflés and baked dishes

Apple bake

	Peel, quarter, core and slice
500 g apples	Beat together
2 eggs	
125 g sugar	When light and foamy, add
1 pkt vanilla sugar	Mix together
125 g white flour	
2 level tsp baking powder	and sieve over the eggs. Layer the apples and topping mixture in a baking dish, finishing with a layer of topping. Bake in a preheated oven.
Electricity:	175–200
Gas:	2–3
Cooking time:	Approx. 30 minutes

> P: 7 g, F: 4 g, Ch: 71 g, kJ: 1485, Kcal: 355.

Accompaniment: Vanilla sauce

Canneloni in savoury tomato sauce

	Plunge
1 kg tomatoes	into boiling water for a moment (do not allow to boil). Remove and plunge into cold water. Peel, cut out ends and dice tomatoes. Peel and finely dice
1 medium sized onion	Heat
2 tbs olive oil	Gently fry the onion in the oil until it is golden. Add the tomatoes together with
1 level tbs tomato purée	Bring to the boil, allow to boil for a moment and season with
salt, pepper	
dried oregano	Stir in
1 tbs chopped parsley	Soak
1 stale bread roll	in cold water. Peel and finely dice
2 medium sized onions	Mix
500 g minced meat (half pork, half beef)	with the squeezed out bread roll, the diced onion and
1 tbs chopped parsley	Season to taste with salt and pepper. Transfer the meat mixture to a piping bag and pipe into
16 uncooked canneloni tubes (bought)	

Put a little of the tomato mixture into a buttered, flat baking dish, lay the canneloni over the base of the dish and distribute the remaining tomato over them. Put

20 g butter — on top in pats and sprinkle with
50 g grated cheese — Bake in a preheated oven
Electricity: 200–225
Gas: 3–4
Cooking time: Approx. 35 minutes

P: 37 g, F: 48 g, Ch: 54 g, kJ: 3510, Kcal: 839.

Tip: Canneloni are a variety of Italian pasta. The word itself means "large tubes", i.e. they are large, hollow tubes of pasta. They are available in the shops, packed in various quantities. Canneloni can be pale in colour or green, in which case they have been coloured with spinach. They are precooked and then stuffed and baked, covered in sauce and grated cheese.

Potato and leek bake

Soak
1 bread roll — in cold water. Peel and finely dice
1 medium sized onion — Mix
500 g minced meat
(half pork, half beef) — with the squeezed out bread roll, the diced onion and season with
salt, pepper — Trim, wash and slice
300 g leeks (prepared weight) — Drain. Put into a buttered baking dish half of
450 g fried potatoes (cold) — Cover with the sliced leeks and season with salt and
dried oregano — Distribute the meat mixture over the top, cover with the remaining potatoes, season with oregano and salt. Mix together
250 ml (¼ l) instant stock (cube)
1 tbs tomato purée — Pour over the ingredients, cover the baking dish and bake in a preheated oven
Electricity: 170–200
Gas: 3–4
Cooking time: Approx. 1 hour

P: 30 g, F: 36 g, Ch: 36 g, kJ: 2580, Kcal: 617.

Pasta bake

	Add
250 g tagliatelle	to
1 ½ l boiling salted water	Stir occasionally and cook al dente in about 8 minutes. Drain on a sieve, refresh with cold water, drain again. Peel
2 medium sized onions	
1 clove of garlic	Dice finely. Heat
20 g butter	Gently fry the onion and garlic in the butter until translucent. Add
500 g minced meat (half pork, half beef)	Fry, stirring continuously and breaking up any lumps (photo 1). Season with
salt, pepper, sweet paprika powder, dried thyme	Plunge
500 g tomatoes	into boiling water for a moment (do not allow to boil). Remove and plunge into cold water. Peel, cut out ends and cut into pieces. Add to the meat (photo 2), cook for about 5 minutes, season with salt, pepper, paprika. Put ⅔ of the pasta into a buttered baking dish, cover with the meat mixture and finish with the remaining pasta. Sprinkle with
100 g grated cheese	(photo 3). Distribute
20 butter	on top and bake in a preheated oven
Electricity:	225 – 250
Gas:	5 – 6
Cooking time:	35 – 40 minutes

P: 39 g, F: 48 g, Ch: 51 g, kJ: 3527, Kcal: 843.

Egg dishes

Fried eggs

	Melt
20 g butter or margarine	in a frying pan. Carefully break
4 eggs	and let them glide into the hot fat to lie next to each other. Sprinkle the egg-white with a little
salt	Fry
Cooking time:	Approx. 5 minutes

P: 7 g, F: 10 g, Ch: 0 g, kJ: 527, Kcal: 126.

Variation: Fry bacon slices in the pan and break the eggs on to the bacon.

Poached eggs

	Bring to the boil
1 l water	
3 tbs vinegar	Carefully break
6 eggs	one at a time into a soup ladle and let them glide into the boiling water (photo 1), turn down the heat (turn off, if burner is electric). When the eggs are cooked, carefully remove them with a slotted spoon (photo 2), immerse them in cold water for a moment, then cut off the edges to make a neat shape
Cooking time:	3 – 4 minutes.
	Serve poached eggs in soup, on toast as a starter, or with a variety of sauces as a main meal.

P: 7 g, F: 9 g, Ch: 0 g, kJ: 368, Kcal: 88.

Tip: Arrange poached eggs on curly endive leaves or serve with mustard sauce.

Egg dishes

Chicken eggs are nutritionally valuable, cheap and versatile. If a recipe calls for "eggs" (without any further specification), chicken eggs are always meant. Other eggs will always be given their full designation, i.e. quails' or gulls' eggs.

The main components of an egg:

Egg yolk
This has a diameter of about 3 cm and is kept in shape by the viscous egg-white and the chalazae. It contains valuable nutrients which make it the most important part of the egg.

Egg-white
This is composed of 4 thin to very viscous layers which surround the yolk. It has an antibacterial effect and provides a measure of protection for the yolk.

Egg shell
As long as it is intact the shell protects the egg from contamination. It is made of an air permeable layer of calcium.

Eggs are categorized according to their freshness and weight. The categories are as follows:
Class **A** fresh eggs: undamaged, clean shell. The enclosed air space should be no higher than 6 mm. No foreign odour. An embryo should not be visibly developed. The egg must be transparent. Eggs up to 7 days old that fulfil these criteria may be sold as **A-extra**.

Class **B**. These eggs need not be as fresh and clean as class A. The air space may have a height of 9 mm.
Class **C**. These are eggs that do not fulfil the specifications of classes A and B and may only be sold for processing in the food industry.

Categorization by weight:
Weight of the individual egg in grammes:

Class	Weight (grammes)
1	70 and over
2	65 to 69
3	60 to 64
4	55 to 59
5	50 to 54
6	45 to 49
7	under 45

Tests for freshness

Floating test

Breaking test

1. A fresh egg

Egg stays horizontal on the bottom

The egg-white is viscous and close around the plump yolk.

2. An egg roughly 7 days old

Egg stands upright

The egg-white is runnier.

3. An egg roughly 3 weeks old

Egg floats

The egg-white is watery and the yolk flat.

Egg dishes

Breaking eggs

Tap the egg firmly against a hard edge and allow it to glide into a bowl. If you are using more than one egg for a dish, each should first be broken into a separate bowl. One bad egg can spoil a whole mixture.

Separating eggs

Tap the egg firmly against a hard edge and break open the shell. Allow the egg yolk to slip from one half of the shell to the other, and catch the egg-white in a bowl standing underneath.

Beating egg-whites

Beaten egg-white is used to lighten up a number of dishes, e.g. soufflés, omelette soufflé, puddings, creams, cakes, etc.
1. The fresher the egg-white the stiffer it will become.
2. Put cold egg-white into a clean, fat-free bowl and beat

with a hand or electric mixer until it is stiff.

Note:
Any trace of yolk or fat will prevent the egg-white from stiffening.

3. Egg-white is stiff when:
   – it stands up in peaks;
   – it can be cut with a knife;
   – it looks dull;
   – the bowl it is in can be turned over slowly without it sliding out.
4. When using beaten egg-white for a recipe, always **fold** it in gently. Never stir, as this would expel the incorporated air and make the consistency of the recipe too firm.
5. If any fatty ingredients have to be added to the beaten egg for flavouring, these should be **folded in** carefully, as otherwise the beaten egg-white will collapse.
6. Use beaten egg-white immediately. It will soon revert to its liquid form if left to stand.

Boiling eggs

1. Prick the blunt end of the egg with a pin or an egg pricker, to prevent it from bursting.
2. Cover with cold water and bring to the boil.
3. Set the egg timer for the desired cooking time as soon as the water starts to boil.
4. Refresh boiled eggs under cold water. This makes them easier to peel.

Note:
If an egg bursts during cooking, add a little vinegar to the water. This binds the protein and stops boiling over.

Cooking times:

Soft boiled eggs	3 – 4 min.
Soft to medium eggs	5 – 6 min.
Hard boiled eggs	8 – 10 min.

Date stamp codes

Egg boxes are stamped with the dates when eggs were packed.

Storage

Eggs store well at room temperature but will keep longer if refrigerated (8 – 10°C).

Eggs with mustard sauce

	Butter 4 ovenproof ramekins. Take
8 eggs	and break 2 into each ramekin. Dice
75 g streaky bacon	and distribute over the eggs. Sprinkle with
salt, pepper	Divide
2 tbs chopped chives	among the ramekins and bake in a preheated oven
Electricity:	200
Gas:	3
Cooking time:	Approx. 25 minutes
	For the mustard sauce, reduce
250 ml (¼ l) double cream (30 % fat)	by boiling in a saucepan. Add
salt	
2 rounded tsp mustard	Loosen the edges of the eggs and upturn on to a serving dish. Garnish with
parsley	Serve the sauce separately

P: 17 g, F: 44 g, Ch: 1 g, kJ: 2105, Kcal: 503.

Tip: Eggs in mustard sauce make a starter for 8, or a main meal for 4 if served with boiled potatoes and salad.

Coddled eggs

	Finely chop
60 g cooked ham	Mix with
40 g grated cheese	Butter 4 cups or coddlers. Take
4 eggs	and break one into each cup (coddler) and cover with the ham and cheese mixture.
	Cover the cups with aluminium foil and stand in hot, not boiling, water until the egg has solidified.
	Arrange washed lettuce leaves on a serving plate and upturn the eggs on to them
Cooking time:	Approx. 30 minutes

P: 12 g, F: 11 g, Ch: 0 g, kJ: 665, Kcal: 159.

Egg dishes

Golden pancakes

	Sieve
250 g white flour	into a mixing bowl. Make a depression in the centre. Beat together
4 eggs	
sugar, salt	
375 ml (⅜ l) milk (3.5% fat)	
125 ml (⅛ l) mineral water	Pour a little of the mixture into the depression and mix in the flour working out towards the edges. Add further egg mixture as needed and make sure no lumps form. In a frying pan heat some of
150 g margarine	Pour a thin layer of batter into the frying pan and fry on both sides until golden. Before turning the pancake, add a little more margarine to the pan

P: 17 g, F: 40 g, Ch: 51 g, kJ: 2766, Kcal: 661.

Accompaniments: Stewed fruit, sugar and cinnamon, maple syrup, fruit.
Variation: Instead of stirring whole eggs into the batter, stir in the yolks and fold in the stiffly beaten egg-white just before cooking. This gives a lighter, more delicate pancake.

Bacon pancakes

	Sieve
250 g white flour	into a mixing bowl. Make a depression in the centre. Beat together
4 eggs	
salt	
375 ml (⅜ l) milk (3.5% fat)	
125 ml (⅛ l) mineral water	Pour a little of the mixture into the depression and mix in the flour working out towards the edges. Add further egg mixture as needed and make sure no lumps form. In a frying pan heat some of
150 g margarine	and fry a few slices of bacon taken from
200 g streaky bacon	until lightly browned. Pour a thin layer of pancake batter over and fry on both sides until golden. Before turning the pancake, add a little more margarine to the pan

P: 26 g, F: 57 g, Ch: 51 g, kJ: 3594, Kcal: 859.

Accompaniments: Green salad.

Boiled eggs

The eggs must be fresh and clean. They must be put into plenty of
water so that the water does not cool off too much when the eggs are put in.

Very cold eggs should be put into warm water first, as they may burst if they are placed in boiling water. Alternatively they may be pricked.

When the eggs are cooked, put them into cold water for a few moments to make them easier to peel

Cooking time: Soft eggs 3 – 4 minutes
Hard eggs 8 – 10 minutes

P: 7 g, F: 6 g, Ch: 0 g, kJ: 368, Kcal: 88.

Apple pancakes

Peel, quarter, core and slice

1 kg soft-fleshed apples For the batter, sieve
250 g white flour into a mixing bowl. Make a depression in the centre. Beat together

4 eggs
25 g sugar
salt
375 ml (⅜ l) milk (3.5 % fat)
125 ml (⅛ l) mineral water Pour a little of the mixture into the depression and mix in the flour, working out towards the edges. Add further egg mixture as needed and make sure no lumps form. In a frying pan heat some of

200 g margarine and fry a few slices of apple in it until lightly browned. Pour a thin layer of pancake batter over and fry on both sides until golden. Before turning the pancake, add a little more margarine to the pan. Sprinkle the finished pancakes with

cinnamon
sugar

P: 17 g, F: 51 g, Ch: 87 g, kJ: 3795, Kcal: 907.

Tip: The pancakes will be lighter if the batter is left to rest for 1 – 2 hours before frying. This allows the flour to swell.

Fluffy omelette with quark filling
(serves 2)

	For the filling, wash and drain
250 g strawberries	Remove their stems and purée them. Mix together
250 g quark (20 % fat)	
25 g sugar	
1 pkt vanilla sugar	
1 tbs lemon juice	Whip
125 ml (⅛ l) double cream	until stiff, fold into the quark, finally fold in the strawberries. For the omelette, beat
3 egg yolks	
grated rind of ½ lemon (untreated)	
30 g sugar	until creamy (photo 1). Beat
3 egg-whites	until stiff and add to the egg cream (photo 2). Sieve
1 rounded tsp cornflour	over, and fold into the egg cream with the beaten egg-white. Melt
30 g butter	in a medium sized frying pan, pour in the batter (photo 3) (you can fry two omelettes if preferred), cover with a lid and cook until the underside is golden brown. Spread the filling on the omelette and fold in half. Serve on a warmed plate, garnished with
strawberries	and sprinkled with
icing sugar	
Cooking time:	Approx. 10 minutes

P: 28 g, F: 48 g, Ch: 49 g, kJ: 3188, Kcal: 762.

Egg dishes

Eggs in chervil sauce

Boil
1 washed bunch of chervil for a few minutes in
375 ml (⅜ l) instant stock (cube) Purée in the food processor. Melt
25 g margarine Stir in
20 g white flour and heat until golden. Pour on the chervil stock and beat with a whisk, making sure no lumps form. Bring to the boil and cook for about 5 minutes. Season to taste with
salt Peel and slice
6 hard boiled eggs Arrange in a warmed dish and cover with sauce

P: 11 g, F: 14 g, Ch: 5 g, kJ: 858, Kcal: 205.

Accompaniment: Buttered boiled potatoes.

Egg fricassee

Drain
200 g cooked mushrooms
175 g cooked asparagus pieces Make up the liquid from the vegetables to 375 ml (⅜ l) with water. Peel
6 hard boiled eggs Slice the eggs and mushrooms. For the sauce, melt
20 g butter or margarine Stir in
25 g white flour and heat until golden. Pour on the
375 ml (⅜ l) prepared liquid Whisk thoroughly making sure no lumps form. Bring to the boil and cook for about 5 minutes. Add the ingredients to the sauce and leave to simmer for about 10 minutes. Beat together

1 egg yolk
3 tbs white wine Fold into the fricassee (do not allow to cook). Season with
salt
lemon juice

Sprinkle with
1 tbs chopped parsley

P: 14 g, F: 15 g, Ch: 8 g, kJ: 1008, Kcal: 241

Variation: Add 1 tsp capers and tiny bread dumplings to the fricassee at the end of the cooking time.
Using up leftovers: Hard boiled eggs can be used for this dish. Rice boiled in stock or with herbs is delicious with egg fricassee.

Scrambled egg

Beat together

6 eggs
6 tbs milk (3.5% fat)
salt Melt
45 g butter or margarine in a frying pan. Pour in the egg and milk mixture. As soon as it starts to set, stir the mixture away from the base and sides of the pan with a spoon. Keep stirring until no liquid is left. Scrambled egg should be crumbly but not dry

Cooking time: Approx. 5 minutes

P: 11 g, F: 19 g, Ch: 2 g, kJ: 971, Kcal: 232.

Variation: Add 3 tsp finely chopped chives to the scrambled egg.

Fruit and desserts

Apple sauce

	Wash, trim and peel
750 g apples	Cut into small pieces and bring to the boil with
5 tbs water	Cook until soft, push through a sieve and add
approx. 50 g sugar	to taste

P: 1g, F: 1g, Ch: 34 g, kJ: 607, Kcal: 145.

Chocolate mousse

	Break
100 g plain chocolate	
50 g milk chocolate	into small pieces, put into a bowl in a water bath (photo 1) and stir over heat until the mixture is smooth. Leave to cool down a little. Beat
3 egg-whites	until so stiff that a cut made with a knife remains visible. Stir in the still warm chocolate (photo 2). Beat
125 ml (⅛ l) double cream (30% fat)	until stiff and fold into the mixture. Refrigerate the mousse for at least 2 hours before serving. Serve with an ice-cream scoop or a tablespoon (photo 3)

P: 6g, F: 22g, Ch: 22 g, kJ: 1289, Kcal: 308.

Accompaniment: Semi-whipped cream.

Tip: The mousse must be well cooled before serving, otherwise it will not have its typical texture. The mousse can be dusted with icing sugar if liked.

Fruit and desserts

A rich supply of foreign and domestic fruit is available throughout the year. The supply varies with the seasons enabling us to ring the changes while taking advantage of low prices. Fruit is high in fibre, vitamins and minerals and should be included in our daily diet. We are familiar with domestic fruit, but the increasing availability of more exotic varieties demands specialist knowledge. The following will provide you with some essential information.

Orange. Available virtually all the year round. Several varieties. If using for fruit salad, peel like an apple, taking care to remove all the white pith. Then cut out the segments so that the membranes are in the centre of the segments. This makes them look fresh and ensures that fibre, which would normally be lost if the membranes are removed, is retained.

Pineapple. Brown, scaly, inedible skin. Ripe fruit is very aromatic, juicy and sweet. The more pronounced the scales are, the more aromatic the fruit is. When the fruit is ripe, the leaves in the crown pull out easily. Unripe pineapple can be stored hung by the crown. Do not store at temperatures under 5°C. The fruit is sensitive to pressure.

Avocado. Pear-shaped fruit. Depending on the variety the skin can be green or brownish-green. Test for ripeness by squeezing gently, it should give a little. Sensitive to pressure. It is best to buy unripe fruit and store at room temperature until ripe. The flesh is yellow and green and the seed is inedible. Overripe fruit is soft and has brown marks.

Figs. Very sensitive fruit with violet, bluish black or slightly grey skin. The flesh is reddish and contains lots of tiny, edible seeds. Only ripe fruit is aromatic. Cannot be stored. Inedible skin. Serve with ham or lamb. Also delicious in fruit salads. Normally sold dried.

Grapefruit. Yellow to orange skin. Yellow or pink flesh. Very juicy, slightly sour, bitter flavour. Can be stored for longer than oranges. Cut fruit through horizontally and eat with a spoon, or squeeze for juice.

Persimmon. Tomato-like fruit with smooth, shiny, orange, inedible skin. Flesh is glassy, slightly translucent and contains 3 – 4 seeds. Ripe fruit is soft and tastes fruity and sweet. Cut persimmon through horizontally and eat with a spoon. Unripe fruit has a felty taste. Suitable for fruit purées or quark desserts.

Cactus fig. Greenish red to yellow fruit with very fine spines and an inedible skin. The yellowish red flesh contains lots of edible seeds. The flavour is fresh and aromatic. Green fruit is unripe. This fruit should be carefully peeled or hollowed out.

Kiwi fruit. Olive brown, slightly hairy, inedible skin. Pale green flesh with edible seeds.

The slightly sour fruit can be peeled or cut in half and the flesh removed, close to the skin, with a spoon.

Lychee. Plum sized fruit with a wrinkled, reddish brown, inedible skin. Pale, juicy flesh with an inedible brownish black seed. Juicy fruit with a sweet and sour, slightly nutty flavour. When the fruit is ripe the skin comes away easily. Available during the winter months.
Mango. Greenish yellow, sometimes reddish inedible skin. Pale yellow juicy flesh. Ripe fruit has a strong aroma and the flesh gives slightly when the skin is pressed. Aromatic, sweet, sometimes tart flavour. The fruit contains a long, flat seed.

Melon. This name covers a variety of fruits with yellow to green, smooth to rough, inedible skins. Juicy, aromatic, sweet flesh, which can be pale yellow to orange. They contain inedible seeds and fibres. Ripe melons give a little when pressed at the stalk end and have a strong aroma.

Papaya. Greenish red or greenish yellow, leathery, inedible skin. Yellow to salmon pink flesh with a sweet flavour similar to that of honeydew melon. Contains a large number of small, inedible seeds.

Good in fruit salads. The fruit is ripe when the skin gives on pressure and turns slightly yellow.

Passion fruit (granadilla).
Greenish yellow or greenish red fruit with a wrinkled, inedible skin. Reddish orange flesh contains lots of edible seeds. Very aromatic, slightly sweet flavour. Ripe fruit has a very wrinkled skin and a strong aroma. Mainly used for drinks.

259

Fruit and desserts

Sweet dishes, whether eaten as dessert or as a main meal, are very popular in Germany. Accordingly there is a wide range of dishes and recipes in this field.

Typical examples of sweet dishes:
- Puddings, blancmanges
- Cream desserts (e.g. thickened with gelatin or cornflour)
- Quark and yoghurt dishes
- Fruit blancmanges
- Fruit salads
- Jellies (e.g. orange or wine jelly)
- Ices (sorbet, ice-cream, parfait, bombe)
- Rice dishes
- Hot sweet dishes (e.g. apple pancakes, crepes, baked sweets, strudel)
- Cakes and biscuits (see Dr. Oetker, Baking for Pleasure)

We would like to take a closer look at a number of the most important sweet dishes.

Pudding
Cold puddings, e.g. for dessert or as snacks.

Hot puddings (cooked in a water bath), e.g. as main meals, perhaps with a soup starter.

The **most common puddings** (blancmanges) use a thickening or gelling agent to thicken the hot liquid (nearly always milk). These puddings also contain sugar and flavouring agents such as vanilla, cocoa, almond or nut. They have to be cooked.

Instant puddings use starch, gelatin or vegetable gelling agents (with pretreated gelling substances) to thicken the **cold** liquid. A large range of puddings, instant, ready prepared and for cooking, is available in the shops.

Making a pudding

1. Boil the milk
2. Mix cornflour/pudding powder with a little cold milk.
3. Stir into the boiling milk, bring to the boil stirring continuously. If the cold mixture contains egg yolk, remove the saucepan from the heat before stirring it in. Return to the heat and to the boil, stirring continuously.

Note:
- If beaten egg-white is to be added to the pudding, it should be folded in to the **boiling** mixture otherwise it will separate.
- Pudding moulds must be rinsed with cold water before the pudding is poured in. This facilitates unmoulding.
- Before unmoulding first loosen the edges.

Fruit salads

Fresh fruit is available all the year round. Only ripe fruit should be used for fruit salad because it is sweet and this means there is no need to add extra sugar. First pour a little freshly squeezed orange or grapefruit juice into a bowl and then mix in the prepared fresh fruit. Instead of putting fruit juice into the bowl, fruit which produces juice, i.e. grapes, melon, etc., can be put in first, before the other fruit is added. The juice is important to help sensitive fruits such as apple and banana to retain their fresh colour.

Gelatin based sweets

e.g. lemon, wine or orange cream, orange or wine jelly. Gelatin is a gelling substance found in the animal protein ingredient collagen. Vegetable based gelling agents are also available. These are produced from seaweed and algae, e.g. agar-agar (normally only available from health food shops).

Gelatin is tasteless and is available in red or white as powder or in sheets. 1 packet of powdered gelatin is equivalent to 6 sheets. To gel ½ litre of liquid you need **6 sheets of gelatin**. For dishes that contain egg yolk (e.g. creams) 1 – 2 sheets less are needed. (If the dish is to be unmoulded, it is advisable to use 1 – 2 sheets more.)

Using gelatin

Powdered gelatin
1. Mix with a little **cold** water and leave to swell for 10 minutes.
2. Dissolve in a water bath or on setting 2 on the automatic burner (12 stage setting).
3. Stir into the mixture that has to set.

Sheet gelatin
1. Soak in plenty of **cold** water.
2. Gently squeeze out the soaked gelatin and dissolve it with a little liquid in a water bath on setting 2 on the automatic burner (12 stage setting).

Or squeeze out firmly and dissolve in a little **hot** liquid.
3. Stir the dissolved gelatin into the mixture that has to set.

Notes on working with gelatin
– Dissolved gelatin should not be stirred into ingredients that are too cold as this can cause lumps to form (e.g. in quark).
– Do not stir fruit into dishes containing gelatin until the mixture has started to set.
– A few exotic fruits, e.g. pineapple, kiwi, mango, must be blanched **before** being used with gelatin. They contain a protein-splitting enzyme that would redissolve the gelatin.

Notes on preparing cream dishes
Cream dishes contain eggs, cream and flavouring agents.
– To ensure a light consistency, the mixture must be beaten until it is white and creamy (about 6 minutes).

– Beaten egg-white or whipped cream should be added to the mixture after it has thickened slightly, otherwise they will rise and settle on the surface.

Fruit blancmanges

To make fruit blancmange, chopped fruit or berries are boiled with fruit juice and thickened with cold mixed cornflour.

Another method of preparing this dish, one that retains the vitamins, is to thicken the juice and then add the fruit to the thickened juice without boiling. This retains the aroma and flavour better, and also the bright colour of the fruit. When frozen fruit is used, the juice needs extra thickening and the frozen fruit must be stirred into the boiling hot juice. Do not bring back to the boil.

Fruit and desserts

Crepes (very thin pancakes)
These are made from a batter containing eggs, milk, double cream or mineral water and flour.

Frying crepes
1. Lightly butter the pan before turning on the heat.
2. Heat pan on setting 1½ – 2 (automatic burner, 6 – 7, gas, medium setting).
3. Pour a little batter into the hot pan and spread it out thinly.
4. Dip a brush in a little oil and brush round the top edge of the pan. The oil will run under the batter.
5. Fry until the crepe can easily be turned. Fry the other side until golden.

6. For the next crepe, pour the batter in **first** and **then** use the oiled brush. If the oil goes into the pan first, the batter will not spread itself as thinly.

Note:
– The batter will be especially light if it is made with mineral water.
– The consistency of the batter is right if it flows when being distributed in the pan.
– Mix the ingredients with a whisk. Using an electric mixer adds air to the batter which has to be expelled to permit the crepes to be really thin.
– The side that is fried first is evenly browned. When serv-

ing, ensure that this is the side facing outwards.

Pancakes

Generally speaking the same principles apply as for crepes. The difference is that the ingredients are mixed to a thicker batter with milk or mineral water and the pancakes are thicker. Other ingredients can be added to the batter before frying, e.g. raisins, chopped nuts or almonds, finely diced apple or berries.

Creamed rice with strawberry sauce

	Bring to the boil
500 ml (½ l) milk (3.5% fat)	with
salt	
50 g sugar	
1 pkt vanilla sugar	Add
100 g round grain rice	Stir, bring to the boil, simmer until cooked, stirring occasionally. The rice grains must still be visible. Leave to cool. Refrigerate. Beat
125 ml (⅛ l) double cream (30% fat)	until stiff. Fold into the cold rice. Transfer the cream to a serving bowl and refrigerate. For the strawberry sauce, wash, drain, trim
500 g strawberries	Purée in the food processor until you have a thick sauce containing small pieces of fruit. Stir in
1 pkt vanilla sugar	
25 g sugar	
Cooking time:	Approx. 20 minutes

P: 8g, F: 15g, Ch: 58 g, kJ: 1703, Kcal: 407.

Tip: Creamed rice with strawberry sauce makes an ideal light lunch on hot summer days.

Pineapple cream

	Drain
4 small slices of tinned pineapple (125 g)	Make up the juice to 375 ml (⅜ l) with water. Mix with
30 g cornflour	
50 g sugar	
1 pkt vanilla sugar	Add 6 tbs of the pineapple juice. Bring the remaining juice to the boil, remove from the heat and stir in the prepared mixture, bring to the boil again for a moment. Stand in a cold place. Stir occasionally. Before the cream has fully set and while it is still lukewarm, stir in
2 tbs lemon juice	Beat
125 ml (⅛ l) double cream (30% fat)	until stiff. Cut the pineapple slices into small pieces, fold the whipped cream and pineapple pieces into the cream, transfer to a serving bowl or individual dessert bowls and refrigerate until it has set slightly

P: 1g, F: 10g, Ch: 29 g, kJ: 887, Kcal: 212.

Yoghurt cream

Mix together

1 pkt powdered white gelatin
5 tbs cold water in a small saucepan, leave to swell for 10 minutes (photo 1). Mix together

1 pot (150 g) yoghurt (3.5 % fat)
125 ml (⅛ l) milk (3.5 % fat)
75 g sugar
1 pkt vanilla sugar
2 tbs lemon juice Heat the gelatin, stirring continuously, until completely dissolved. Add 2 tbs of the yoghurt mixture (photo 2), stir then pour into the remaining yoghurt mixture. Stand in a cool place. Beat

125 ml (⅛ l) double cream (30% fat) until stiff. When the yoghurt mixture starts to thicken, fold in the whipped cream (photo 3). Refrigerate

P: 5g, F: 13g, Ch: 25 g, kJ: 1017, Kcal: 243.

Tip: This cream can be prepared several hours in advance. Serve with sugared fruit or puréed fruit sauces.

Fruit and desserts

Quark cream
(cooked)

Mix

1 pkt vanilla sauce powder (or
custard powder) with
20 g cornflour
2 egg yolks 6 tbs taken from
375 (⅜ l) cold milk (3.5%) Bring the remaining milk to the boil with
25 g butter, salt Stir the powder into the milk, which has been removed from the heat, return to the burner, bring to the boil for a moment, stand in a cold place, stirring occasionally. Mix together

250 g low fat quark
75 g sugar until smooth. Stir in the cold cream by the spoonful. Add
rum flavouring to taste. Beat
2 egg-whites until stiff, carefully fold into the quark cream, transfer the cream to a glass serving dish and garnish with

10 g grated chocolate

P: 15g, F: 13g, Ch: 35 g, kJ: 1339, Kcal: 320.

Lemon cream

In a small saucepan mix together

1 heaped tsp white powdered gelatin
3 tbs cold water Leave to swell for 10 minutes. Beat
2 egg yolks
2 tbs hot water until foamy. Gradually beat in
75 g sugar Keep beating until you have a creamy mixture. Stir in
5 tbs lemon juice
grated rind of ½ lemon (untreated) Heat the gelatin, stirring continuously, until completely dissolved. Add 3 tbs of the egg yolk mixture, stir in and then beat the gelatin into the remaining egg yolk mixture. Stand in a cold place. Beat
2 egg-whites until stiff. Beat
125 ml (⅛ l) double cream (30% fat) until stiff. When the egg cream starts to thicken, carefully fold in both ingredients (keeping back a little whipped cream for decoration). Transfer the cream to a serving bowl or to in-

dividual dishes. Refrigerate until set, decorate with the reserved whipped cream and

4 halved maraschino cherries

P: 5g, F: 13g, Ch: 21 g, kJ: 937, Kcal: 224.

Tip: This cream can be prepared the day before, so that only the cream for decoration needs whipping before the dessert is served.

Almond pudding with apricots
(serves 6)

	Quarter
250 g dried apricots	Stew until soft in
125 ml (⅛ l) water	
25 g sugar	Leave to cool off, drain. Prepare a vanilla and almond pudding as described on the packet. Leave to cool off, stirring occasionally to prevent a skin from forming. Beat
250 ml (¼ l) double cream (30% fat)	until stiff, stir into the cold pudding. Add the quartered apricots. Transfer to individual dishes and chill

P: 6g, F: 17g, Ch: 51 g, kJ: 1607, Kcal: 384.

Stewed pears

	Peel, cut in half and core
500 g pears	Bring to the boil
250 ml (¼ l) water	
50 g sugar	
1 pkt vanilla sugar	When boiling, add the pears and cook until soft. Leave to cool off and add
sugar	to taste

P: 1g, F: 0g, Ch: 29 g, kJ: 510, Kcal: 122.

Variation: Boil 1 piece of cinnamon and 3 cloves with the pears.

Fruit and desserts

Whipped wine cream

Put

1 egg yolk, 60 g sugar
125 ml (⅛ l) dry white wine

into a saucepan. Over a water bath beat the mixture with an electric mixer on lowest setting, until it is light and foamy throughout (it must roughly double in volume – do not allow to boil)

P: 3g, F: 3g, Ch: 16 g, kJ: 510, Kcal: 122.

Stuffed baked apples

Wash but do not peel

8 medium sized apples

Remove the cores with an apple corer (photo 1), working from the flower end and taking care not to pierce right through the apple. Arrange the apples in a buttered baking dish or on small, ovenproof plates (photo 2). Mix together

1 – 2 tbs butter
1 – 2 tbs sugar
1 pkt vanilla sugar

Stuff the apples with this mixture. A little rum can be poured into the baking dish if liked. Cook in a preheated oven until soft

Electricity: 200 – 225
Gas: 3 – 4
Cooking time: 30 – 45 minutes

P: 0g, F: 3g, Ch: 18 g, kJ: 406, Kcal: 97.

Tip: Ground or split almonds or raisins soaked in rum can be added to the butter sugar mixture before the apples are stuffed.

Fruit and desserts

Fruit salad
(serves 6)

	Peel, quarter and core
2 medium sized apples (250 g)	Peel, cut in half and remove stone from
1 small mango (250 g)	Wash, dry, cut in half and remove stone from
1 nectarine (75 g)	
1 medium sized peach (75 g)	Peel and separate into segments
1 medium sized orange (150 g)	Peel and slice
1 kiwi fruit (50 g) 1 banana (150 g)	Wash and drain
100 g strawberries	Remove stalks, cut into pieces. Mix the fruit with
3 tbs lemon juice	
30 g sugar	Serve the fruit salad in a glass bowl. Sprinkle with
30 g chopped walnuts	

P: 2g, F: 4, Ch: 26 g, kJ: 607, Kcal: 145.

Accompaniments: Whipped cream flavoured with egg flip or instant vanilla pudding.

Real fruit blancmange
(serves 6 – 8)

	Wash, drain, remove stalks and stones from
300 g sour cherries	Wash, drain, strip from stalks
300 g redcurrants	Wash, drain
300 g raspberries	Mix the berries with
100 g sugar	
3 peeled bitter almonds	Bring to the boil in a saucepan and boil for about 15 minutes. Mix together
300 ml sour cherry juice	
30 g cornflour	Stir into the fruit, bring to the boil, leave to cool. Remove the almonds before serving

P: 29g, F: 1, Ch: 39 g, kJ: 685, Kcal: 164.

Delicious with vanilla sauce or vanilla flavoured whipped cream.

Tip: Use frozen or preserved berries instead of fresh ones.

Vanilla sauce

	Prepare vanilla sauce from a packet, using
30 g sugar	
500 ml (½ l) milk (3.5% fat)	Leave to cool off, stirring occasionally. Beat
125 ml (⅛ l) double cream (30% fat)	until almost stiff and fold into the cold sauce

P: 5g, F: 14, Ch: 18 g, kJ: 941, Kcal: 225.

Tip: Vanilla sauce is the perfect accompaniment to fruit blanc-manges, fruit salads, baked apples, hot apple cake and apple strudel.

Stewed gooseberries

	Top and tail and wash
500 g gooseberries	Bring to the boil
125 ml (⅛ l) water	
100 g sugar	Add the gooseberries and cook until soft (do not stir). Leave the fruit to cool off and sweeten with
sugar	if liked.

P: 1g, F: 0, Ch: 36 g, kJ: 644, Kcal: 154.

Tip: When stewing fruit, it is important that the fruit is not cooked to a pulp. For many varieties it is sufficient to bring them to the boil and then leave them to barely simmer in a covered pan.

Redcurrants with cornflakes

	Wash, drain well and strip
375 g redcurrants	Mix the fruit with
50 g sugar	Leave to stand to allow the juice to collect. Divide among 4 dessert bowls. Just before serving sprinkle each bowl with
2 tbs cornflakes (30 g)	Mix
2 pots yoghurt (150 g each) (3.5% fat)	and pour over the cornflakes

P: 5g, F: 3, Ch: 31 g, kJ: 724, Kcal: 173.

Microwave

Ossobucco

	Wash and dry
4 slices of shin of calf (about 200 – 300 g each)	Rub with
salt	
pepper	Brush with
cooking oil	Trim, wash and finely chop (photo 1)
1 onion, 1 carrot	
1 slice of celeriac	
1 leek	Braise the vegetables in a covered glass dish with
2 tbs oil	for 5-6 minutes on 100. Preheat browning dish for 7-8 minutes on 100. Put the meat into the browning dish (photo 2) and fry on both sides for 3 minutes each on 100. Mix the vegetables with
2 tbs tomato purée	
grated lemon rind	
sage, thyme, rosemary	
1 clove	
1 crushed clove of garlic	
125 ml (⅛ l) white wine	
125 ml (⅛ l) instant stock (cube)	Stir well and pour over the meat (photo 3), cover and microwave for 4 – 6 minutes on 100, continue cooking for 20 – 30 minutes on 70. Remove the meat from the sauce, season to taste and stir in
a little double cream or crème fraîche	Return the meat to the sauce and serve
Total cooking time:	approx. 45 minutes

P: 35 g, F: 17 g, Ch: 8 g, kJ: 1536, Kcal: 367.

Accompaniment: Spaghetti with Parmesan cheese and salad.

Microwave

Before you start cooking with your microwave oven, you must remember that it is different to cooking in a normal oven. The difference starts with the cooking utensils. All types of container that will allow the microwaves to pass through to the food are suitable. These include ovenproof glass (not crystal), china (this should be undecorated and should not have a gold rim, the colours used for decorating china can contain metal), earthenware and heatproof plastics. We highly recommend AEG's MICROTHERM cookware for microwave cooking.

Your specialist retailer will also stock browning dishes for microwave ovens and these can normally also be purchased from the oven manufacturer (photo: MICRO-browning dish).

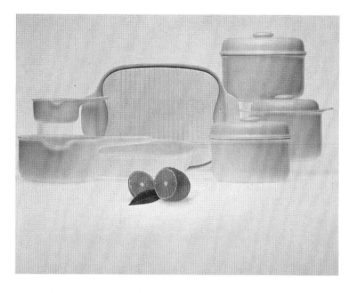

must take care to ensure that the dish is at least 2 cm away from the side walls of the oven and that the sides of the dish are no higher than 2 cm. All metal or metal coated cookware is unsuitable for use with microwave ovens. Metal reflects microwaves and prevents cooking from taking place. Some ovens come with a

food thermometer. This is very useful for checking liquids and large pieces of meat.

Practical tips

All food being cooked in a microwave oven should be covered, either with the corresponding lid or simply with a plate. This accelerates

Aluminium dishes can also be used to some extent in microwave ovens. Many convenience foods are sold in aluminium dishes. They can be reheated in these dishes but you

heating up and stops food from drying out. This is especially important for long cooking times. All food should be stirred, turned or rearranged occasionally during cooking. This evens out any differences in temperature. The door of the microwave oven can be opened at any time because the oven automatically switches off and will not switch back on until the door has been shut again. When thawing or cooking irregularly shaped food (e.g. poultry or fish), the flatter or thinner parts can be covered with aluminium foil for the last few minutes of thawing or cooking. The aluminium foil must be kept at least 2 cm away from the inside walls of the oven and must not touch them. Cooking times depend mainly on the quantity of food to be cooked, but are also dependent on the type and texture of the food. One rule of thumb which is useful to remember says: **double quantity = double cooking time.**

Power settings

Setting 100% (corresponds to approx. 700/600/500 watts)	– Highest setting. To start cooking: boiling, browning, braising etc.
Setting 60 – 70% (corresponds to approx. 500/450/400 watts)	– Finishing meat that has been browned on setting 100. For reheating delicate foods.
Setting 40 – 50% (corresponds to approx. 350/300/250 watts	– To continue cooking soups, casseroles, baked dishes, pasta (after starting on setting 100). – Braising food that has been browned.
Setting 30% (corresponds to approx. 230/200/180 watts	– Thawing meat, fish, fruit, bread and cake.
Setting 15 – 20% (corresponds to approx. 140/120/100 watts	– Warming cold dishes or beverages. – Thawing fatty food. – Proving yeast dough. – Thawing cream and butter.

Microwave

Savoury pork fillets

	Preheat a browning dish for 7 – 8 minutes on 100. Wash, dry and skin
1 fillet of pork (about 400 g)	Rub with
1 tsp salt, 1 tsp sweet paprika powder	Brush with
1 tbs cooking oil	Put into the browning dish and brown, turning frequently. Peel and dice
2 onions	Add to the meat, cover and microwave for 5 – 7 minutes on 100. Remove the meat from the browning dish, slice. Put
1 pkt frozen peas (about 300 g)	into a glass dish. Season with
salt	Add
25 g butter	Cover and microwave for 7 – 8 minutes on 100. For the sauce, mix together
1 pot (125 g) yoghurt (full fat)	
1 tsp sugar, grated lemon rind (untreated)	
2 – 3 tbs lemon juice	
1 small glass of spirit	Stir into the pan juices. Arrange the meat slices fanlike in the pan, filling the intermediate spaces with peas and
2 slices chopped pineapple (tin)	Cover and heat for 4 – 7 minutes on 100
Total cooking time:	Approx. 20 minutes

P: 25 g, F: 22 g, Ch: 20 g, kJ: 1703, Kcal: 407.

Roast pork

	Wash and dry
800 g pork (from the neck)	Rub with
salt	
pepper	
paprika powder (sweet)	
ground caraway	
rosemary if liked	
garlic powder	
1 – 2 tbs oil	Slice
½ onion	and put it into a glass dish. Put the meat on to the dish on an up-turned saucer or on a micro grid and cook for 8 – 10 minutes on 100. Turn the meat over and microwave for 25 – 35 minutes on 70 – 60 (food thermometer shows 80 – 85C.) Remove the

meat from the microwave oven and from the glass dish. Cover and leave to stand for 5 – 10 minutes. For the sauce, mix the pan juices with

a little water	Mix together
1 level tbs white flour	
2 tbs cold water	or
1 tbs gravy thickener	Stir into the pan juices and boil for 1 – 2 minutes on 100. Stir once during cooking. Slice the meat and serve with the gravy
Total cooking time:	Approx. 45 minutes

P: 36 g, F: 19 g, Ch: 2 g, kJ: 1435, Kcal: 343.

Accompaniments: Boiled potatoes and salad.

Tip: If you want the meat to look darker when cooked, sprinkle it with paprika and/or curry powder before cooking, or brush with a little mushroom soy sauce.

Irish Stew

	Wash, dry and dice
500 g lamb	Microwave in a glass dish for 10 – 14 minutes on 70 – 80. Peel and dice
1 onion	Scrape, wash and dice
1 carrot	Cut into strips
500 g savoy cabbage (prepared weight)	Peel, wash and dice
200 g potatoes	Add the onion and vegetables to the meat, season with
salt	Cover and microwave for about 10 minutes on 100. Add
300 g frozen peas	
1 tsp thyme	
1 bay leaf	Stir, cover and microwave for 30 – 40 minutes on 50, stirring occasionally. Remove the dish from the microwave oven and leave to stand, covered, for 5 – 10 minutes. Sprinkle with
1 – 2 tbs chopped parsley	
Total microwaving time:	Approx. 60 minutes

P: 32 g, F: 23 g, Ch: 26 g, kJ: 1950, Kcal: 466.

Roast beef with horseradish sauce

	Preheat browning dish for 6 – 8 minutes on 100. Wash and dry
800 g rump	Brush with
cooking oil	Season with
salt	
pepper	Put the meat into the browning dish and fry for 5 – 6 minutes on 100, turn and microwave for a further 7 – 8 minutes on 100 (food thermometer 50°C, medium) (photo 1). Remove the beef from the oven, cover and leave to stand for 10 minutes. For the horseradish sauce, remove the crusts from
30 g white bread	Soak in a glass bowl (photo 2) in
125 ml (⅛ l) white wine	Stir in
2 tbs horseradish (from a jar)	
1 tsp mustard	
1 tbs sour cream	Season to taste with
salt	
sugar	Microwave for 2 – 3 minutes on 100, stirring once during cooking. Stir in
1 egg yolk (photo 3)	Microwave for a further minute on 70 – 60. Serve the sauce with the roast beef
Total cooking time:	Approx. 15 minutes

P: 40 g, F: 27 g, Ch: 6 g, kJ: 2000, Kcal: 478.

Accompaniments: Fried potatoes or chips, fine vegetables.

Turkey drumsticks braised with vegetables

	Peel and finely dice
1 onion	Remove the white inner walls and seeds from
½ green pepper	Wash and cut into strips. Wash, dry and quarter
2 tomatoes	Put all the vegetables into a glass dish. Wash and dry
2 turkey drumsticks (about 1 kg)	Season with
salt	
pepper	Add to the vegetables with
30 g melted butter	Cover and microwave for about 15 – 18 minutes on 80 – 70. Remove the meat from the dish. Add
250 ml (¼ l) water	
1 pkt instant gravy powder	to the vegetables, return the turkey to the dish with its other side up. Cover and microwave for 50 – 70 minutes on 50. Remove the turkey from the dish, cut the meat from the bones, cut into chunks. Pass the sauce through a sieve and season with
salt	
sugar	
sweet paprika powder	Put the meat and vegetables into a glass dish. Sprinkle with
50 g grated cheese	Microwave for 4 – 6 minutes on 100
Total cooking time:	Approx. 1 ½ hours

P: 46 g, F: 18 g, Ch: 5 g, kJ: 1636, Kcal: 391.

Accompaniments: Rice and salad.

Tip: The cooking times depend on the initial temperature and consistency of the food.

Rabbit in thyme sauce

	Wash, dry and cut into pieces
approx. 1 kg rabbit	Mix together
2 tbs cooking oil	
salt	
1 tsp sweet paprika powder	Brush the meat with this mixture. Peel
1 onion	Put into a glass dish with the meat, cover and microwave for 4 – 6 minutes on 100. Turn the meat and microwave for a further 30 – 40 minutes on 50.

Remove the dish from the microwave oven and the rabbit from the dish, leave to cool. When cold cut the meat from the bones and chop. For the thyme sauce, make up the pan juices to 250 ml (¼ l) with

water	Pour into a glass dish and stir in
2 tbs white flour	mixed with
4 tbs cold water	or
2 tbs gravy thickener	Season with
½ tsp finely chopped thyme	
salt	
1 – 2 tbs lemon juice	Add
2 tbs milk	
2 tbs double cream	
2 tbs white wine	Cover and microwave for 3 – 5 minutes on 100, stirring once during cooking. Add the meat to the sauce, adjust the seasoning if necessary and reheat for a further 2 – 3 minutes on 100
Total cooking time:	Approx. 1 hour

> P: 53 g, F: 29 g, Ch: 5 g, kJ: 2255, Kcal: 539.

Accompaniments: Rice and salad.

Braised mushrooms
(serves 3)

	Peel and finely dice
1 onion	Put into a glass dish with
20 g butter	Cover and sauté for about 3 – 4 minutes on 100. Wash and slice
500 g fresh mushrooms	Add to the onion, cover and microwave for about 12 – 15 minutes on 100. Add
125 ml (⅛ l) sour cream	
salt	
1 – 2 tsp lemon juice	Add
1 tsp white flour	mixed with
2 tsp cold water	or
1 tsp instant thickener	to the mushrooms, cover and microwave for a further 3 – 4 minutes on 100, stirring once during cooking. Sprinkle with
chopped parsley	
Total cooking time:	Approx. 18 minutes

> P: 6 g, F: 13 g, Ch: 8 g, kJ: 728, Kcal: 174.

Accompaniments: Roast meat, meatballs or bread dumplings.

Szegediner goulash

	Wash, dry and cut into cubes (photo 1)
500 g pork	Put into a glass dish with
1 tbs sweet paprika powder	
1 tsp Worcester sauce	
salt	Cover and microwave for 10 – 14 minutes on 70 – 80. Peel and finely dice
1 onion	With a fork, loosen
500 g tinned sauerkraut	(photo 2). Mix with the meat (photo 3) and add
500 ml (½ l) instant stock (cube)	Cover and microwave for about 5 minutes on 100. Continue cooking for 20 – 25 minutes on 70 – 50, stirring occasionally. Season to taste with
salt, sweet paprika powder	Remove the Szegediner goulash from the microwave oven, cover and leave to stand for 5 – 10 minutes
Total cooking time:	Approx. 40 minutes

P: 29 g, F: 5 g, Ch: 6 g, kJ: 828, Kcal: 198.

Accompaniments: Mashed potato

Onion soup
(serves 6)

	Peel and slice into rings
2 large onions (about 400 g)	Put into a dish with
50 g margarine	Season with
salt	
pepper	Cover and microwave for 6 – 10 minutes on 100. Divide the onion rings among 6 soup bowls. Mix together
500 ml (½ l) hot instant stock (cube)	
125 ml (⅛ l) white wine	Divide the liquid among the soup bowls. Toast 2 slices of white bread, cut into small cubes, add to the onion soup and sprinkle with
50 g grated cheese	
cayenne pepper	Put the bowls into the microwave oven and microwave on 100 for 10 – 14 minutes, until the cheese has melted
Total cooking time:	Approx. 20 minutes

P: 4 g, F: 10 g, Ch: 10 g, kJ: 665, Kcal: 159.

Tip: Cookware suitable for microwaving is made from: glass, earthenware, china, heat resistant plastics. Unsuitable: containers made from metal or decorated with paints containing metal (gold edge/decoration).

Zucchini with dill

	Wash (peel and deseed large ones)
500 g zucchini	and cut into ½ cm thick slices. Put into a glass dish with
salt	
20 g butter	Cover and microwave for 8 – 12 minutes on 100, stirring occasionally. Wash and chop
1 bunch of dill	Add to the zucchini with
1 tbs chives	
3 tbs double cream	Adjust seasoning and reheat for a further minute on 100
Total cooking time:	Approx. 10 minutes

P: 3 g, F: 8 g, Ch: 9 g, kJ: 527, Kcal: 126.

Braised savoy cabbage

	Wash and cut into strips
1 savoy cabbage (approx. 750 g)	Peel and finely dice
1 onion	Put into a glass dish with
3 tbs cooking oil	Cover and microwave for 3 -4 minutes on 100. Add the vegetables to the onions with
125 ml (⅛ l) water	
salt	
white pepper	
4 – 6 crushed juniper berries	
1 tsp stock powder	Microwave for 5 – 7 minutes on 100, stir and continue cooking for 15 – 30 minutes on 50. Add
125 ml (⅛ l) double cream	Cook for a further 2 – 3 minutes on 100. Remove the cabbage from the microwave oven, cover and leave to stand for 5 – 10 minutes
Total cooking time:	Approx. 30 minutes

> P: 5 g, F: 21 g, Ch: 8 g, kJ: 1033, Kcal: 247.

Tip: Vegetables cooked in a microwave oven retain their crispness and fresh colour.

Sauerkraut in wine
(serves 2)

	Dice
25 g streaky bacon	Peel and finely dice
1 onion	Put both ingredients into a glass dish, cover and microwave for 2 – 3 minutes on 100. With a fork loosen
300 g tinned sauerkraut	Add to the bacon and onion with
1 tsp sugar	
125 ml (⅛ l) white wine	Cover and microwave for 12 – 16 minutes on 100. Remove from the microwave oven and leave to stand for 5 – 10 minutes
Total cooking time:	Approx. 15 minutes

> P: 4 g, F: 9 g, Ch: 129 g, kJ: 761, Kcal: 182.

Serve sauerkraut in wine with roast pork or roast pork knuckle.

Rice and meat casserole

	Preheat the browning dish for 6 – 8 minutes on 100. Peel and finely dice
1 onion	Wash, dry and cut into cubes
500 g pork	Put into the browning dish with the onions and
cooking fat	Cover and fry for 5 – 7 minutes on 100 (photo 1), stirring occasionally. Dice
500 g skinned tomatoes (photo 2)	and add to the meat with
1 tsp paprika powder	
1 tsp tomato purée	
100 g rice	
125 ml (⅛ l) water	Bring to the boil in 7 – 9 minutes on 100 and continue cooking for a further 20 – 25 minutes on 60 – 70. Remove from the microwave oven, cover and leave to stand for 5 – 10 minutes. Sprinkle with
chopped parsley	
grated cheese	(photo 3)
Total cooking time:	Approx. 40 minutes

> P: 31 g, F: 10 g, Ch: 25 g, kJ: 1389, Kcal: 332.

Accompaniments: Mixed salad.

Microwave

Fried egg

	Preheat browning dish for 2 minutes on 100. Add
1 tsp cooking oil	to the browning dish. Break
1 egg	into the oil and microwave for 1 – 2 minutes on 60. If you want to cook more than 1 egg at a time, the cooking time per egg is increased by ½ – 1 minute. (Use 1 tsp cooking oil per egg)
Total cooking time:	Approx. 1 – 2 minutes

P: 2 g, F: 4 g, Ch: 0 g, kJ: 420, Kcal: 104.

Scrambled egg
(serves 1)

	Beat together
2 eggs	
salt, pepper	
a little mineral water	Pour into a buttered glass dish and microwave for 1½ – 3 minutes on 100 until set, stirring occasionally and scraping the egg mixture away from the base of the dish
Total cooking time:	Approx. 2 minutes

P: 14 g, F: 16 g, Ch: 19 g, kJ: 900, Kcal: 215.

Tip: Whole eggs should not be cooked in the microwave oven as their shells could burst.

Farmhouse breakfast
(serves 2)

	Preheat browning dish for 4 – 5 minutes on 100. Peel and dice
1 onion	Add to the browning dish with
50 g diced streaky bacon	Microwave for about 1 minute on 100. Peel and slice
400 – 500 g boiled potatoes	Mix together
3 eggs	
125 ml (⅛ l) milk	
3 – 4 tbs double cream	

salt Add with the potatoes to the onion and bacon in the browning dish. Cover and microwave for 8 – 12 minutes on 100. Turn the potatoes a few times during cooking

Total cooking time: Approx. 10 minutes

P: 19 g, F: 36 g, Ch: 39 g, kJ: 2431, Kcal: 581.

Rice pudding

Wash

150 – 200 g round grain rice Put into a glass dish with
750 ml (¾ l) milk
½ tsp salt
30 g sugar
untreated lemon rind Cover and bring to the boil in 8 – 12 minutes on 100. Continue cooking for 25 – 30 minutes on 30. Remove the dish from the microwave oven, cover and leave to stand for 10 – 15 minutes

Total cooking time: Approx. 40 minutes

Note: If preparing half the quantity, note the following times: bring to the boil in 6 – 7 minutes on 100, continue cooking for 15 – 20 minutes on 30. Leave to stand for 10 – 15 minutes.

P: 9 g, F: 7 g, Ch: 51 g, kJ: 1314, Kcal: 314.

Pasta (spaghetti, tagliatelle, etc.)

In a longish glass dish bring to the boil
1 l salted water in 12 – 14 minutes on 100. Put
250 g pasta into the boiling water, cover and microwave for 3 – 5 minutes on 100, stir and continue cooking for 8 – 14 minutes on 50. Remove the pasta from the microwave oven, drain, refresh with
cold water Before serving, reheat for a further 3 – 5 minutes on 100 with a little
butter, salt

Total cooking time: Approx. 20 minutes

P: 8 g, F: 2 g, Ch: 45 g, kJ: 1017, Kcal: 243.

Microwave

Ocean perch (red fish) with vegetables

	Wash, dry and cut into portions
400 g ocean perch fillets	Sprinkle with
lemon juice	
salt, pepper	
sweet paprika powder	Place in a low sided glass dish, cover and microwave for 6 – 8 minutes on 100. Turn the fish half way through the cooking time. Drain
250 g cooked peas and carrots	
250 g cooked asparagus	
200 g cooked mushrooms	and add to the fish with
20 g butter	
125 ml (⅛ l) double cream	Microwave on 100 for 8 – 10 minutes. Sprinkle with
1 bunch chopped parsley	
Total cooking time:	Approx. 20 minutes

P: 24 g, F: 18 g, Ch: 119 g, kJ: 1331, Kcal: 318.

Szegediner style fish goulash

	Peel and finely dice
2 onions	Dice
20 – 30 g streaky bacon	Put into a glass dish with
2 – 3 tbs cooking oil	Cook for 4 – 5 minutes on 100. With a fork, loosen
300 g tinned sauerkraut	Add to the onions with
70 g tomato purée (1 small tin)	
125 ml (⅛ l) instant stock (cube)	Cover and microwave for 4 – 6 minutes on 100. Continue cooking for 10 minutes on 70. Wash, dry and cut into cubes
500 g cod fillet	Season with
juice of 1 lemon	
salt, pepper	
soup seasoning	Add to the sauerkraut, cook for 4 – 6 minutes on 100
Total cooking time:	Approx. 30 minutes

P: 24 g, F: 16 g, Ch: 6 g, kJ: 1180, Kcal: 282.

Accompaniments:	Boiled potatoes.

Cocoa
(serves 1)

	Put
250 ml (¼ l) milk	into a glass and heat for 2–3 minutes on 100 (food thermometer, approx. 75°C), remove from the microwave oven. Stir in
2–3 tsp instant cocoa powder	

P: 9g, F: 9 g, Ch: 16 g, kJ: 770, Kcal: 184.

Irish coffee
(serves 1)

	In a glass, heat
4–5 cl whisky, 1 tsp sugar	for 20–30 seconds on 100. Remove from the microwave oven. Add
1 cup hot, strong coffee	Top with
1 tbs whipped cream	

P: 19g, F: 6 g, Ch: 6 g, kJ: 1393, Kcal: 333.

Grog
(serves 1)

	Bring to the boil
1 tea glass of water	in 1 ½–2 minutes on 100. Remove from the microwave oven. Heat
1 glass of rum	for 30 seconds on 100, add to the water and sweeten with
sugar	

P: 0g, F: 0 g, Ch: 109 g, kJ: 481, Kcal: 115.

Mulled wine
(serves 1)

	Heat
1 tea glass of red wine	
1–2 cloves, ½ stick of cinnamon	for 1–1 ½ minutes on 100. Sweeten with
sugar	

P: 0g, F: 0 g, Ch: 14 g, kJ: 577, Kcal: 138.

Tip: It is advisable to use the thermometer to check the temperature of beverages which have been heated in the microwave oven.

Fillets of plaice with sweet corn and mushroom sauce

	Wash and dry
500 g fillets of plaice	Sprinkle with
3 tbs lemon juice	
salt	Wash and drain
300 g sweetcorn (tin)	Drain
200 g cooked mushrooms	Slice thinly and put into a glass dish with the sweet corn (photo 1). Pour
125 ml (⅛ l) dry red wine	over. Knead together
30 g butter	
1 tbs white flour	Add the kneaded butter to the vegetables (photo 2), microwave for 5–7 minutes on 100, stir, place the prepared fish on the vegetables and microwave for 5–7 minutes on 100. Carefully stir in
3–4 tbs double cream	
chopped parsley	(photo 3)
Total cooking time:	Approx. 10 minutes

P: 26 g, F: 12 g, Ch: 19 g, kJ: 1326, Kcal: 317.

Accompaniments: Boiled potatoes and salad.

Tip: Whole fish takes longer to cook than fillets of fish.

Cream caramel

Mix together

100 g sugar
2 tbs cold water Put into a glass dish and caramelize for 4–6 minutes on 100,
stirring occasionally (photo 1) to ensure that it browns evenly.
Stir in

4 tbs hot water Mix together
40 g cornflour
500 ml (½ l) milk
20 g sugar
1 pkt vanilla sugar Stir into the caramel (photo 2). Bring to the boil in 5–7 minutes
on 100, stirring frequently during cooking. Remove from the
microwave oven and leave to cool. Beat
125 ml (⅛ l) double cream until stiff, fold into the caramel mixture (photo 3). Chill
Total cooking time: Approx. 12 minutes
Sprinkle with chopped, browned almonds.

P: 5 g, F: 14 g, Ch: 48 g, kJ: 1148, Kcal: 346.

Tip: Stir sweet dishes containing, semolina, sago, rice, cornflour or
pudding powder frequently during cooking to prevent lumps
from forming.

Quark pudding

	Stiffly beat
3 egg-whites	Mix together
250 g low fat quark	
30 g semolina	
3 egg yolks	
50 g sugar	
50 g butter	
20 g ground nuts	
30 g washed sultanas	
½ tsp baking powder	Fold in the beaten egg-whites. Butter a glass baking dish and sprinkle with
ground nuts	Pour in the quark mixture, level the top and microwave for 10 – 12 minutes on 50 and for 2 – 4 minutes on 100. Serve while still warm with fruit sauce and whipped cream.
Total cooking time:	Approx. 12 minutes

P: 17 g, F: 31 g, Ch: 38 g, kJ: 2134, Kcal: 510.

Tip: Use high dishes when preparing puddings so that the liquid (i.e. milk) cannot boil over.

Roquefort toast

	Preheat the micro-grill plate for 2 – 3 minutes on 100. Butter
4 slices white bread	Cover with
4 slices boiled ham	
4 half pears (tinned)	
1 tsp cranberry jelly	
100 g Roquefort cheese	Heat on the micro-grill plate for 2 – 3 minutes on 100 until the cheese has melted
Total cooking time:	Approx. 5 minutes

P: 18 g, F: 19 g, Ch: 19 g, kJ: 1381, Kcal: 330.

Tip: When gratinating dishes with cheese, set short cooking times, as cheese will run. Give an extra few seconds or minutes if needed.

Hawaii toast

	Preheat the micro-grill plate for 2−3 minutes on 100. Butter
4 slices white bread	Cover with
4 slices boiled ham	
4 slices tinned pineapple	
4 slices cheese	Heat on the micro-grill plate for 3−4 minutes on 100 until the cheese has melted
Total cooking time:	Approx. 5 minutes

P: 21 g, F: 16 g, Ch: 22 g, kJ: 1364, Kcal: 326.

Mushroom toast

	Preheat the micro-grill plate for 2−3 minutes on 100. Butter
4 slices white bread	Drain
200 g cooked mushrooms	Slice and mix with
8 tbs grated cheese	
4 tbs chopped parsley	Season with
salt	
pepper	Put the mushroom mixture on the bread and heat on the micro-grill plate for 4−5 minutes on 100
Total cooking time:	Approx. 4−5 minutes

P: 5 g, F: 8 g, Ch: 12 g, kJ: 167, Kcal: 40.

Snails

	Place
12 frozen snails	on a snail dish. Pour
3 tbs white wine	over. Heat for 2−4 minutes on 70. Serve with French bread
Total cooking time:	Approx. 4 minutes

P: 5 g, F: 0 g, Ch: 1 g, kJ: 167, Kcal: 40.

Index by chapters

Meat

Venison and Game

Poultry

Vegetables

Salads

Casserole dishes

Potatoes and cereal products

Soufflés and baked dishes

Egg dishes

Fruit and desserts

Microwave

Alphabetical Index of chapters